Gossamer Days

Gossamer Days

Spiders, Humans and Their Threads

Eleanor Morgan

First published by Strange Attractor Press 2016

Including hardcover edition of 250 featuring a print by Eleanor Morgan and a cover image depicting a sand drawing from Malakula, Vanuatu after Mr C.O. Waterhouse.

Design and layout by Tihana Šare and Mark Pilkington

ISBN 978-1-907222-35-9

Strange Attractor Press

BM SAP, London, WC1N 3XX, UK

www.strangeattractor.co.uk

Printed in the UK

For R.E.R.

Spider goats

Mary Pfeiffer's
Spider Room

Folly Island

Nora Songer's
Spider Farm

Continuous
Weaving

Spider Island

Cobweb paintings

Nyastaranga

Voice
Disguisers

kite fishing

Spider Web
fabric

Spider farm
and
Spidery

Author's note:
The text is divided by the eyes of *Araneus diadematus.*

The threads that touch seem the same, but the extremes are distant, as when, often, after a rainstorm, the expanse of the sky, struck by the sunlight, is stained by a rainbow in one vast arch, in which a thousand separate colours shine, but the eye itself still cannot see the transitions. There, are inserted lasting threads of gold, and an ancient tale is spun in the web.

Ovid, *Metamorphoses*

Contents

List of Colour Plates

Introduction

In the late summer of 2004 I began to collect the silk of spiders. These are the gossamer days, the time of year when every bush, railing, gap and crevice seems to sparkle with threads of spider web. I lived in the basement of a damp two-storey wooden house in Vancouver. My windows were partly submerged in mud, framing an underground world of worm tunnels and ants' nests pressed up against the glass. Surrounded by activity, I wanted a material to make with. I collected cobwebs from the window frames and used the individual threads of silk to create drawings by positioning them on a piece of black cloth. They were dull things, flattened, dusty, without the glow of a spider's web. I began to experiment with ways of suspending a thread of silk between two points, to catch the light. I hooked it, wound it, glued it, and licked it, until finally I had attached each end of a single strand of silk to the wall using superglue. It had taken me all day.

The image I held in my mind was a sculpture made from spider silk. I did not know what form it would take, but I knew what it would *do* — it would glow and it would be fantastical. To make it I needed to collect bright silk, not grey cobwebs.

In the early hours of the morning, when the spiders had freshly spun their webs, I walked through the parks and streets with my silk-collecting equipment. This consisted of ten rectangular frames made from balsa wood, stored inside an empty popcorn box. If I saw a spider web I positioned one of my wooden frames behind the web and slowly drew it towards me until the silk threads attached themselves tightly to the frame, each one a small canvas. When all the frames were full, I returned to my basement, extracted the individual strands of silk and wound them around a small loom. The silk was more attracted to human skin than to metal needles or tweezers, so my fingers became my clumsy tools, weaving and catching the silk threads, too delicate to feel, and invisible to me unless the light shone at a certain angle. Hoping that I was still holding the threads I waved my fingers in the air around the loom, until the weave appeared to tighten.

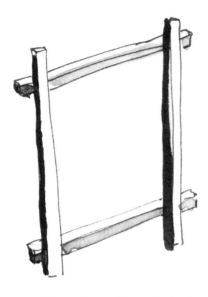

It was a sticky, time-consuming business and I soon found a more efficient method. In the local park, spun inside the huge leaf of a Gunnera plant, was a web with the spider sitting to one side. As I began to pull and wind the web onto my wooden frame I felt an unfamiliar resistance. I looked at the spider. Its abdomen and back legs were raised towards me. I realised that the silk I was winding onto the frame was still attached the spider's silk-producing spinnerets. Gently turning the wooden frame, I was able to wind a few metres of fresh, dry silk directly from the spider's body before she cut the thread with her back legs.

It was a still, sickening moment, to sense the physical, bodily resistance of another animal along the thread of silk to my fingers — as if I were unravelling a spider from the inside. It marked the point at which my interest in creating a fantastical glowing object was replaced by a fascination with the spiders themselves. As I collected silk I gradually learned more about the spiders' behaviour. I knew at what time they would probably be weaving their webs (early in the morning), what kind of environment and bushes they preferred (slightly shady), and their tendency to eat the silk I had already collected — a morning's work could be lost in a matter of seconds if a spider strayed onto the reel of silk. Back in my apartment, the slow work of weaving and staring at spider silk strayed into my dreams, in which the lines, my fingers and the spiders regularly appeared.

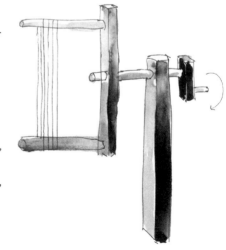

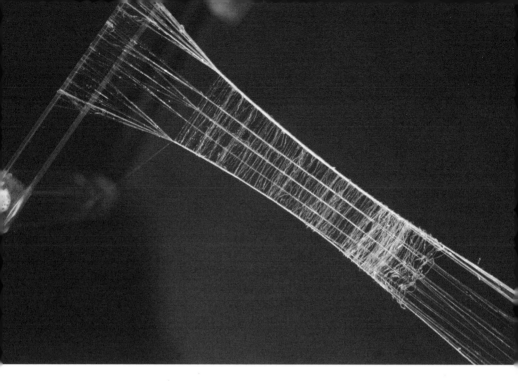

Spider silk on loom

I began to identify the different spiders not by their taxonomic names (that came later) but by their appearance and the quality of their webs. I watched them as they caught a fly, lifting their rear into the air and pulling from their spinnerets numerous threads with which they bundled their prey. My way of walking and the paths I chose were now guided by the opportunity to see spiders whether or not I was gathering silk. I tried to keep in time with the spider's rhythm of making — to attune to the spider. I developed certain rules of collecting: I would not disturb a spider if it was eating, or if it was in the process of building its web, or if its web was structurally astonishing, stretching metres between the trees. I even started giving them dead flies in exchange for the silk. They ignored these, preferring living prey.

At the time, it felt like a private discovery. But without realising it, I had become part of a long history of humans collecting spider silk. This obscure activity stretches back centuries and across cultures. Spiders and their silks have mapped the stars, created fabrics, made music and healed our wounds. 'If a simple wound in the flesh be fresh

... a spider's web cleansed of dust may be put on, it cures the wound because it cleanses and consolidates', wrote the fourteenth century English cleric John Mirfield. Spider web is a material close to hand, and its properties are so extraordinary that material researchers are now exploring ways to create an artificial version that could be used to regrow damaged tendons and nerves.

This book is about the wonderful and varied uses of spider silk and the humans and spiders involved. More generally, it is about making things and how materials and what we do with them are tied up with how we think.

Spiders are renowned as animals that many people find terrifying, myself included. I don't like touching them, or the surprising way that they move suddenly and quickly. Why do they cause such fear? They are not particularly dangerous to humans — out of around 34,000 species only a couple can inflict severe illness from a bite, and very occasionally death. Instead, it seems to have something to do with the idea that a spider is malevolent; it has a plan, and it's watching and waiting to carry it out. As one man responded when I told him about my interest in spiders, 'I know they're out to get me'. Alongside this fear is admiration that such a creature can weave forms of delicate beauty, and produce a material from its body that is typically described as being stronger than steel. For the pre-Socratic philosopher Democritus, all human art originated in our learning from and imitating the processes of animals, 'in the most important things we became learners: of the spider in weaving and healing, of the swallow in building, of the songbirds — swan and nightingale — in imitative song', and according to Seneca, our attempts can never match those of the spider: 'Do you not see how the spider weaves a web so subtle that man's hand cannot imitate it'.

Fear, admiration and perhaps slight envy; such feelings towards spiders and their silk have affected the ways that humans have used the material, but they are not universal responses. Across cultures, different attitudes to spiders are entangled with different ways of making and how an object is valued. The tendency in western cultures is to value finished objects, to put a price on them and to preserve them. In other cultures, such as in the islands of Vanuatu in the South Pacific, value lies not in the physical object, but in knowing what it means and how it is made.

This secret knowledge is protected and handed down through generations, while the object itself may be transformed or even destroyed and remade. In this region a certain species of spider and its web is honoured because it represents the continuous cycle of life and death.

Spiders remake their webs, eating the old web and creating the new, sometimes every night. Their continuous making is useful for spider silk collectors, but it has been a particular frustration for cultures that like their objects to be finished, preserved and displayed. How do you preserve a spider's web? This is exactly the question faced by museum conservators dealing with artefacts made from spider silk. In gardens and homes, spider webs are blown away by the wind or removed with dusters and vacuum cleaners. Inside the museum, they are carefully protected and preserved.

I am drawn to spiders because, like me, they make things. There is no strict order to this — making something does not begin with an isolated idea that comes from nowhere, which I then apply to a material, moulding it to my will. Rather it is a combination of materials, techniques, and ways of thinking. And added to these is the role of other animals and what they make. Spiders have evolved to deal with extremes of temperature and a range of environments, so that species can be found on every continent. In particular, they have evolved to spin silk and produce silks with different properties. The stories in this book are therefore not just about human practices; they are about the spiders and how the process of making things is linked across species.[1] This approach involves leaping across some historical divides that have been remarkably resilient since Aristotle first constructed them over two thousand years ago: that human making is different from that of all other animals because we are the only animals with reason, we make with an idea in mind. This definition of human making is an awkward trap, because it is not simply saying that the way humans make things

---

1 Although this book focuses on human uses of spider silk, there are other animals that collect and use spider silk for their own constructions. The long-tailed tit builds its nest from a combination of spider webs, moss and twigs. Because of the elasticity of spider silk, the bird's nest will expand as its young hatch and grow. Some species of hummingbird use dry threads of spider silk to lash together twigs for their nest, and even tie down pebbles as weights to stop the nest from tipping.

is different to spiders, which is different to beavers, bees, swallows, sticklebacks and mussels. It's saying that there is a special kind of making which is found only in humans. Our making is cultural, while that of all other animals is natural.

These imaginary boundaries between human and animal worlds are untenable given the disastrous effects of human activity on the environment, but they also limit us imaginatively. Making is not only human; we are part of a much larger mess of organisms that are, right now, making and unmaking forms, materials and worlds. Our connection to these worlds is not just because we share the same space or materials, it is because to be alive is to make, to form environments that in turn form ourselves.

Spiders are particularly productive animals, of silk, myths, superheroes and creation tales. Instead of exploring all these spidery associations, the focus of this book is on the spider silk objects themselves and how and why they were formed. Without exception, they are made from the silk of female spiders. This may be because female spiders are more visible than the males — they are larger and make larger webs — but it is also associated with specific male and female roles in human society. Certain spidery activities are the preserve of women, while in some cultures they are forbidden to participate or even know how spider silk objects are made. In spite of the huge number of spider species, only a few are involved in the history of humans collecting spider silk. In northern climates, this has tended to be the silk of the European garden spider, *Araneus diadematus*, while in tropical regions it is the silk of the golden orb spiders, *Nephila*, and the wall crab spiders, *Selenopidae*. With so few spiders, and yet such a variety in how their silk has been used, it is possible to compare how these spiders are perceived and different approaches to making.

The stories of spider silk collectors stretch back to the origins of language, storytelling and making. They are 'clues', a word that comes from the Anglo Saxon *cliwen* meaning both a ball of yarn and a silk cocoon: a gathering of human and animal threads to be traced.

The following tales are about what happens when one making animal meets another.

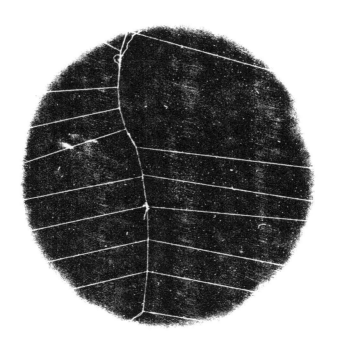

Beginnings

Spiders cohabit with us, trailing their other reality
through and across our rooms and thoughts
A.S. Byatt

This morning, between the arm of my deckchair and a dead stalk of Evening Primrose, a female European garden spider, *Araneus diadematus*, sits on the edge of her web. It is early autumn and she is at her largest, having shed her exoskeleton eight times since the spring, when she emerged from a silken egg sac along with hundreds of her siblings. Any injury she has sustained over the year, such as losing a leg, has been repaired through the shedding and regrowth of her outer skeleton. Her body is almost spherical, about the size of a broad bean, and comes to a slight point at the bottom of her abdomen. If you look closely, here are her spinnerets — the organs through which she pulls and spins her silk.

Her web is the archetypal orb web featured in Halloween decorations. From a distance it appears as a circle with spokes and spiralling threads, but on closer viewing the spiral is formed of straight lines that converge towards the centre. She has secured the web to its surroundings by strong guy ropes of silk. From point to point, the web stretches over a metre in diameter.

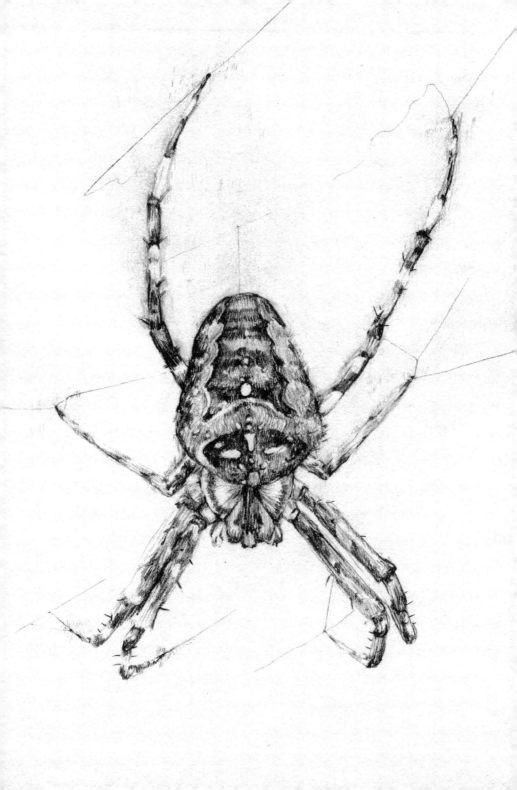

Beginnings

At the moment, clasped between her legs and jaws is the body of a Flesh fly; a large black and white fly whose signature red eyes are no longer visible. Only seconds before, the fly had become entangled in the sticky threads. Its panicked buzzing carried across the web to the spider sitting beneath a leaf. Sensing the vibrations, she immediately dropped from her hiding place and immobilised the fly by injecting it with poison and wrapping it with a fan of silken threads that she pulled from her spinnerets with her legs. Intermittently she bites it with her fangs, adding some digestive fluid from her intestines so that the fly is liquefied and she can suck it into her body (see colour insert: Fig 1).

The silk with which she bundles the fly is her *aciniform* silk, and is just one of seven different silks that she can produce, each with different properties and uses. The silks are formed as a liquid within the spider's silk glands, and travel through the silk ducts from where they emerge through her three pairs of spinnerets. She can move these spinning organs independently, synchronising their twisting and turning. If we could look closer, we'd see that these spinnerets end in thousands of 'spigots', the tubes through which the silk emerges. The silk cannot be propelled out of her body, rather it must be pulled out. She can use her legs to pull at the thread or she can attach it to an object such as a leaf and walk away from it, with the thread extending behind her. When we say that a spider 'spins' its silk, this is what we mean — the pulling action through which spider silk liquid transforms into a strong and elastic thread.

The spider has finished wrapping her prey and carries it off to a dead leaf to continue eating. During the day, she waits here and is almost invisible, for she is the same light brown colour as the leaf. Running the length and width of her back are small white dots, which give her the colloquial name 'cross spider'. She keeps a constant check on her web with an outstretched leg resting on a signal line of silk. Any vibrations, of passing prey or predator, will travel through the strands of the web to this signal line, and to the audio-vibratory sensors in her leg. In response, she can swiftly move onto the web to catch her prey, or hide from any danger.

← *Araneus diadematus*

5

If the web is badly damaged or if it has become too visible because of dust and fly carcases she will rebuild it, often waiting until nightfall so that she does not become prey to any passing birds. She eats her old web and with it any leftover prey still entangled in its threads. She does this quickly, her eight legs working to bundle the silk into her jaws. Full of energy from this recycled protein, she prepares to make a new web.

She raises her body with her back legs, and points her spinnerets into the air. A passing breeze catches a strand of silk and pulls it into a long thread. The silk wafts around in the wind until it hits an object — an iron railing, a branch, or a dozing human. She pulls the thread and secures it to make a tightrope. She then walks across this bridge of silk, making another silken line as she goes. When she reaches halfway, she drops down, creating a vertical line that she attaches to another object. She now has her basic 'Y' shaped structure. The meeting point of the three lines in the 'Y' shape will form the centre of her web. They are the guy ropes, keeping the web taut.

So far, she has used two types of silk to make the web: the cement-like *piriform* silk to stick the threads together, and the dragline or *major ampullate* silk to create the threads. Out of her seven types of silk, only two are sticky. Dragline silk is dry, strong and elastic. This is the silk that a spider produces behind it when it walks, and the type that I collected on my silk collecting frames. It is one of the toughest natural materials on Earth. Run your fingers along one of the strands that links a spider web to its surrounds — it is not easy to break.

The spider's next task is to make the radiating spokes that link the centre of the web to its edges. She moves back and forth from web frame to hub. Each time she returns to the centre she tugs at the thread she has made, checking its tension. This tugging action might also be a way of measuring where the next line should go — each angle is carefully measured from the previous spoke.

The web now looks a bit like the wheel of a bike. It has a frame and spokes. The next bit is to add the sticky spiral threads. But if she did this straight away, the spokes would sag under her weight and the web would lose its tension. So she makes a temporary spiral of threads starting from the centre using a third type of silk produced from her *minor ampullate* gland.

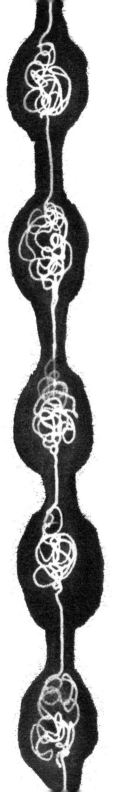

These are quite widely spaced, but will exist only briefly as something to hang on to while she adds the permanent sticky strands.

It has taken the spider five minutes to get to this stage, but the next process will take her at least twenty minutes. Before she begins, she will rest for a moment.

Working from the edge, she starts to lay down a spiral of capture threads. This sticky silk is a combination of silks from two glands: the *flagelliforme*, which forms the centre of the thread, and the *aggregate*, which forms the outer coating and sticky droplets.[2] When these two materials are combined, the viscous coating arranges into evenly spaced droplets along the thread and these act like windlasses by gathering the threads of flagelliform silk into sticky bundles. It is highly elastic and able to extend by up to five times its normal state. Working in tandem with the threads of tough dragline silk, this stretchiness means that the web will be able to withstand the force of a flying insect without breaking — and most importantly it can do this without pinging the insect back into the air like a trampoline. Instead, the web can stretch and then immediately return to its original shape and tension.

The creation of the sticky spiral is perhaps the most mesmerising part of the process. At each spoke the spider pulls and fixes a thread from her body with a little wiggle of her abdomen and tests

---

2 Not all spiders make sticky silk. Some create what are called 'cribellate' threads, which are crimped, puffy threads almost like Velcro, in which flies become entangled.

the tension by tugging it with her leg as she goes. She stops short of the centre. Here, at the meeting point of dry threads she will hang, head towards the ground. With each leg on a radiating thread, the web is an extension of her body allowing her to sense any movement in her surroundings. In less than half an hour she has built a new web, and will repeat this action every few days.

If you see a European garden spider on its web, it's highly likely to be female. Although males also spin silk, they are smaller and tend to wander around looking for, or sniffing out, females. Once he has reached sexual maturity he will stop spinning the sticky capture threads and will only live for one more week, during which he must find a female. Late summer is mating time, and you may be lucky enough to see some extraordinary courtship behaviour.

Before beginning his search, the male garden spider will make a tiny triangular web a few millimetres in length. On to the web he deposits a drop of semen from a genital opening on the underside of his abdomen. He now has to transport this to a female using specially adapted organs called palps. These look like a pair of very short legs attached to either side of a spider's head. In females, palps are used for sensing and handling prey. In the male, palps are like bulbous syringes that suck up and store semen while he searches for a female.

Each spider species has its own method of courtship. When he finds a female, a male garden spider will spin a thread of silk and attach it to the female's web. He will then pluck the thread like a guitar string. It's important that he gets this serenade right, in particular the spacing between the notes which are specific to each species of spider. If he gets the tune right, she might mate with him. If he gets it wrong, he will become her next meal. Even if she recognises him as a potential mate, their mating appears as a dangerous (and very leggy) process — if he is injured at all, she will make good use of his protein by eating him — fuel for the energy needed to grow their offspring. After all, he has not long to live.

Spider sex organs
Top: Epigyne of female *Araneus diadematus*
Bottom: Male palpal organs of the spider family *Araneidae*

If his serenade is successful, the male will insert his engorged palp into her epigyne, the genital opening on the underside of her abdomen. Here he deposits the semen, and to prevent any other males mating with her he then 'plugs' the epigyne by breaking off the end of his palp. She will store the semen until it is time to fertilise her eggs.

The female spider beside me has already mated. Sometime during the next month she will spin a silk cocoon into which she will lay her eggs using her seventh type of silk — *tubuliform* silk. This will keep the eggs warm and protected. She will die before winter comes.

For spider watchers, late spring is an exciting time. This is when the egg sacs of the garden spider break open and hundreds of spiderlings emerge. They gather as a pulsating circle of tiny orange balls. With the slightest disturbance of the web they appear to explode — scattering outwards in all directions before returning to the centre. Eventually they will have to find their own space, or they will become prey to their siblings. To do this, a spiderling will raise its abdomen and release a thread of silk that will be pulled and spun by the wind. It will let go with its legs and the breeze will carry it off to a new settlement. This is known as ballooning. A spiderling can land anywhere. This surrender to the breeze means that spiderlings are often the first creatures to inhabit newly formed islands. As the warmth of spring arrives, hundreds of spiderlings balloon through the air, coming to rest when the breeze drops or the silk attaches to a passing obstacle. The seventeenth century scientist Robert Hooke observed these fine threads floating through a fog and 'catching several of those and examining them with my microscope, I found them to be much of the same form, looking most like to a flake of worsted produc'd to be spun, though by what means they should be generated, or produc'd, is not easily imagined'. It seems likely, he wrote, that these threads form the 'great white clouds, that appear all the summer time'. It is as if the strands produced by the ballooning spiders in the spring gather together to create the puffy clouds of summer skies.

Once the spiderlings have landed they spin their first web.

This process of making seems instinctive — an evolutionary learning, rather than that of an individual. Yet there is evidence that an individual spider may learn over its lifetime how to create better webs. In a recent study, zoologists found that as individual orb-weaving spiders age, they create webs that are larger below their centre. These asymmetrical webs improve the chance of catching prey because a spider can more quickly drop down the web to grab entangled prey than climb up it. This suggests that rather than being entirely instinctive, a spider learns and changes its web building through experience.

European garden spiders are one of the major spinners in this book. Perhaps thanks to Spider-man, their circular orb-web tends to be the one we imagine when we think of a spider web. However, all spiders produce silk and unlike other silk-producing animals, such as silkworms, they are able to produce silk throughout their lifetime.

The ancestors of today's spiders probably used silk to protect themselves and their eggs. This ability then developed into a mechanism for hunting and capturing insects. Unlike the spider, insects could fly. How could a creature without wings catch them? A great diversity of webs has evolved to deal with this problem. Some are like nets, others are like pulley systems, swinging balls or secret trapdoors that resemble mediaeval weaponry. It is a continuous game of entrapment and evasion. The great diversity of insects that now exist may in part have evolved in response to the increasing diversity of spider silk traps, which themselves adapted in response to the evolution of insects.

The net-casting spider *Deinopidae* doesn't spin an orb web; instead it hangs upside down and holds a small net of silk between its legs. It has particularly large eyes — giving it an appearance that has led to its other name, the ogre-faced spider. When it senses prey it leaps at it, expanding the net, and covering and capturing its victim.

The bolas spider *Mastophora* holds a line of silk with a globule of sticky glue at the end. It then releases a pheromone similar to that of moths, which attracts them to its bolas. As the moth approaches, the spider swings its sticky ball and reels in its catch. These spiders are also noted for their ability to mimic their surroundings; to avoid predators some species of bolas spider adopt the appearance of bird droppings.

Corolla spiders *Ariadna* live in the Namib Desert in southern Africa in vertical tube holes burrowed into the sand. They select quartz crystals and place them in a circle around the entrance to their burrow. The spider then attaches a strand of silk to each of the crystals, sits in the burrow, and places its legs on the other end of the threads of silk. If passing prey touches a crystal, even slightly, the resulting vibrations will carry through the crystal and down the silk to the spider's sensory hairs on its legs. It is not known why the spider chooses quartz out of all the other surrounding stones, but both quartz crystals and spider silk are piezoelectric. This means that the application of any pressure to these materials results in an electric charge — which can be carried through both materials to the spider in its burrow. This effect would not be possible with other stones found in the spider's environment. It is therefore possible that the spider deliberately chooses quartz for its piezoelectric properties.

Like the garden spider, other species also use their silk in courtship and mating. The male of the spider genus *Pisaura* captures a fly, wraps it in silk, and presents it to the female. If she accepts the fly, the male can mate with her with less chance of being eaten by the female. During mating they may both take a break to snack on the fly, or even continue to munch on the fly while entangled.

Offering food to the female seems a practical strategy for avoiding being eaten. Other species use silk during mating in ways that may seem to have similar practical aims, but are revealed to have what zoologists term 'symbolic significance'. The male crab spider *Xysticus* ties down the larger female with his silk so that she appears to be entirely immobilised and unable to attack him. However, as soon as they have finished mating, the female easily frees herself from the silken ties. Similarly, the male of the *Nephila* spider is tiny in relation to the female. Before mating with her, he will place a few strands of his silk over the female's legs. The purpose of these ties is therefore not to prevent the female from moving, but perhaps is similar to the gentle leg stroking that many spider species use during mating — it may simply be pleasurable.

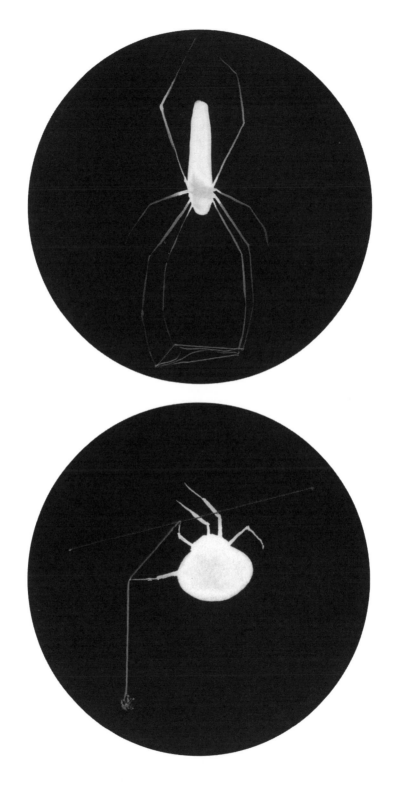

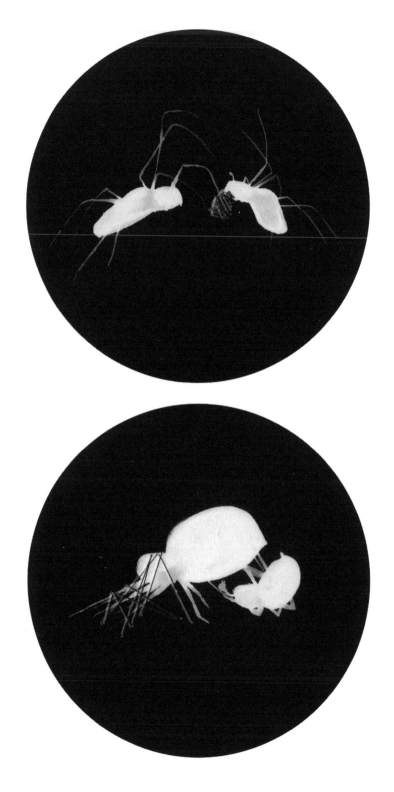

Spider silk is therefore not just one material. The European garden spider has seven silks to choose from and the properties of these differ from silks produced by other species of spider. Silk properties are fairly similar among the same species, but even these can differ depending on what and how recently the spider has eaten, its age, the outside temperature, the environmental humidity, and the weight of the web — increased, for example, by the number of flies hanging on it. Spider silk alters according to its maker and environment.

The association between a spider's diet and its web was shown in a bizarre experiment carried out in the 1950s. A German pharmacologist, Peter Witt, was contacted by a zoologist friend who wanted to photograph orb-weaving spiders building their webs. The problem was that these spiders tend to make their webs at night or the early hours of the morning, when he would rather be asleep in bed. He asked Witt if it was possible to make the spiders build their webs at a more convenient time by drugging them. Witt accepted the challenge and began to experiment with feeding different drugs to the spiders. He fed the spiders amphetamines, marijuana, caffeine and LSD. None of these had any effect on the time of day that the spider built its web, but it did have some strange effects on the web the spider produced. On speed or marijuana, the web was recognisable as an orb-web, but with a few threads missing. But on caffeine, the orb-web structure was

Spiders on drugs. Left image: normal web. Right image: web made by spider on caffeine © NASA

almost unrecognisable — irregular with large gaps between the threads. Only one drug improved the regularity of the spider's web building: LSD.

Although Witt did not succeed in changing the web building time of the spiders, he had a possible tool for identifying the type and quantity of drugs taken by humans, by feeding samples of urine to the spiders and classifying the resulting webs. This was never developed, perhaps in part because it would have required a lot of patience and the assistance of a large number of spiders — one in the corner of every police interrogation cell.

I've been using words interchangeably for the material that spiders make: cobweb, spider web, gossamer and spider silk. Each term evokes a different type of material — dirty or wondrous.

The earliest recorded word in English for a spider's thready material is 'cobweb', which appears in written texts in the fourteenth century. The word 'cob' means 'head' and is an abbreviation of 'attercoppa', an Old English word for a spider that means 'poison head'. A cobweb is a dusty material, the stuff that accumulates in attics, sheds and under the stairs, surrounding the rooms in which we live. Inside the house they are proof of slovenly housekeeping, a room disused, a mind lost. Even the spiders have abandoned these webs.

The word 'web' has an older lineage, with roots in Indo-European words meaning to weave, while the word 'spider' stems from old northern European words meaning to spin. Web and weave, spider and spin. These associations between human uses of threads and the name for a spider web suggest that the activity of spiders was recognised as analogous to that of humans. This is significant, because such links are not found in the words for other silk spinning creatures, such as caterpillars, or for animals whose silk or wool has been used for centuries as a weaving material, such as silkworms or sheep. The words seem specifically associated with an *action* rather than a material: web is 'woven' and spider is 'spinner'. Like the weaver at her loom, the spider follows a repetitive rhythm and movement to combine its threads.

'Gossamer' has a more obscure history. It possibly stems from the Middle English word for late summer, a time in which geese were in season ('goose-summer') and when spiders are at their most productive. It seems to be a word better whispered than said — the long 'ss' like a buzzing, with the heat, sex and laze of a late summer. In Dylan Thomas's *Under Milk Wood* the village schoolmistress, Gossamer Beynon

> *high-heels out of school. The sun hums down*
> *through the cotton flowers of her dress into the bell of*
> *her heart and buzzes in the honey there and couches and*
> *kisses, lazy-loving and boozed, in her red-berried breast.*
> *Eyes run from the trees and windows of the street,*
> *steaming 'Gossamer', and strip her to the nipples and the bees.*

Gossamer is not the deathly web of a 'poison head' but the delicate touch and glint of a magical material.

The term 'spider silk' appears in the early eighteenth century. It signals a shift in how spiders were perceived — not just as animals that wove their webs, but as producers of a material that might be useful to human industry. During this period, the first attempt to harvest and weave with spider silk took place in France in an effort to compete with the silkworm industry. 'Spider web' was too spidery a term for the extracted threads that could be woven on a loom. It was therefore given the name of the material that it most resembled in appearance, behaviour and potential use: silk.

As the following chapters reveal, the story of humans collecting spider silk is full of such moments of enthusiastic confidence at the industrial potential of these animals, followed by despair when faced with the difficulty of dealing with the spiders themselves.

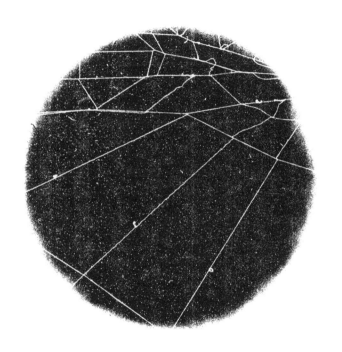

Lining

'A line is length without breadth'
Euclid

Spider silk fills in spaces, joining leaves to posts and branches to buildings. Wherever she goes, the European garden spider leaves traces of her path so thin that they appear as glances of light. If these threads could be sealed within a box they would remain indefinitely; the record of an animal's movement within a particular place and time.

In a storage room at the Smithsonian Museum in Washington, D.C., among rows of antique telescopes, is a small wooden box containing a circular brass ring known as a micrometre. Used to measure the angle of the stars, this particular micrometre was once fixed inside the eyepiece of a large telescope at the United States Naval Observatory. At its centre is a hole containing a grid of adjustable lines running horizontally and vertically. These are spider lines: silken threads spun by orb-weaving spiders over a century ago.

If we travelled along one of these spider silk threads we would eventually meet a hardened bead of shellac, another arthropod material,

↑ Micrometre, late nineteenth century
(Photo courtesy of the Smithsonian Institution.)

→ Detail of micrometre, showing the spider lines
(Photo courtesy of the Smithsonian Institution.)

produced by the female lac bug whose sticky excretions are scraped from the bark of trees to form a multipurpose lacquer and glue. The shellac secures the spider line to metal gears, which are attached to the outside edges of the micrometre. Using these gears, each of the individual spider lines can be moved upwards or downwards, and their position can be recorded. In its sealed box in the museum, the micrometre is carefully protected from dust and from the curiosity of human fingers — viewed at certain angles the spider lines disappear and so could be unwittingly broken in a moment. The box must also be spider-tight, as the silken lines would be eaten in seconds by a spider wandering along the museum shelves.

The Smithsonian's micrometre is one of the few remaining examples of a once-common practice. For over three hundred years the threads of spiders stretched across the eyepieces of telescopes, microscopes, land-surveying instruments and gun-sights, allowing the human observer to shrink vast distances to the accessible size of a spider's web. This largely unnoticed and forgotten practice began when a spider spun its web inside a telescope tube and changed the course of astronomical and terrestrial measurement forever.

Spiders have a tendency to be drawn to dark nooks and crevices, and telescopes are particularly attractive places to spin. In the early 17th century William Gascoigne was one of a group of astronomers based in the north of England. One night he looked down the eyepiece of his telescope and saw two things in perfect focus: a star and lines of spider silk. A spider had spun its web only a few inches from the eyepiece, yet both the web and a star billions of miles away appeared in perfect focus. How was this possible? By chance, the spider had positioned its web across a specific point inside the telescope, known as the common focal plane. This is where the light focused through the eyepiece lens and the objective lens meet. Anything positioned at this point can be seen in focus with the object viewed through the telescope — such as a star. In a letter to a fellow astronomer, Gascoigne gave credit for this discovery to God who directed the actions of the spider to reveal to him 'the unexpected knowledge'. It signalled the beginning of a competition of lines, between the astronomer's desire to find the perfect line of measurement and the spider's creation of threads that are all too real in their bodily and sticky presence.

The spider web inspired Gascoigne to invent the first micrometre. At its centre was a reticule, a cross of threads or lines that derives from the Latin word *reticulum*, meaning a net or meshwork bag. Gascoigne made the reticule by crossing two human hairs inside the eyepiece. He could position the centre of these hairs onto the star he was observing, and then measure the angle of his observation using the gears of the micrometre. Until Gascoigne's invention, astronomers had mapped the movement of the Earth and planets by observing the change in their appearance over short periods of time. By introducing lines of measurement into this observation, Gascoigne had created a miniaturised model that transposed the scale of the universe to the size of a human hair. Plucked from his head, these hairs were far easier to handle than spider silk, and the glass lenses during this period were not of sufficient magnification or clarity to require anything thinner.

Over the following century, various materials in addition to human hair were used to create reticules, such as silkworm silk, metal wires or brass plates. These were sufficient for the thick, bubbly glass lenses of the instruments. Yet, as the lenses developed, so did their magnification — and the human hairs, silkworm silk and metal wires appeared neither straight enough nor sufficiently fine for the required observation and measurement. The astronomer William Herschel wrote of the problem in 1782, while attempting to measure the distance between two stars: 'I have in vain attempted to find lines sufficiently thin to extend them across the centres of the stars, so that their thickness might be neglected. The single threads of the silkworm, with such lenses as I use, are so much magnified that their diameter is more than that of many of the stars'.

It was not just a problem of thickness. To provide an accurate line with which to measure, the material had to remain constant. Metal wires, for example, changed in thickness with the temperature and humidity of the environment. The wires were also in danger of breaking or sagging in response to vibrations. A finer, and more reliable, material was needed. In the late eighteenth century a number of individuals, oblivious of William Gascoigne's spider experience, independently discovered that spider silk might be the perfect material. A Tuscan physiologist, Felice Fontana, used spider lines in a levelling instrument, while an American instrument maker, David Rittenhouse, reported, 'I have lately with no small difficulty placed the thread of a spider in some of my instruments, it has a beautiful effect, it is not one tenth of the size of the thread of a silkworm, and is rounder and more evenly of a thickness. I have hitherto found no inconvenience from the use of it, and believe it will be lasting, it being more than four months since I first put it in my transit telescope, and it continues fully extended, and free from knots or particles of dust.'

The properties of spider silk made it the perfect material. It is thin, so does not obstruct what is being observed, it is able to withstand extremes of temperature without sagging, and it can be fixed taut and straight within the eyepiece. As one spider line maker described, spider silk is formed of strands so fine they 'cannot be seen by eye'. Even under the magnification of strong lenses, the spider lines did not obscure the stars, or add any unwanted thickness to the line of measurement. They were the perfect line, defined by Euclid, the founder of Classical geometry, as a 'breadthless length' — a line without any material weight.

By the mid-nineteenth century, spider lines were in common use in large telescopes. In his history of the Royal Observatory at Greenwich, the nineteenth century astronomer Edward Maunder described the process of mapping the stars with spider lines:

'The watcher who wishes to observe the passing of a star must note two things: he must know in what direction to point his telescope, and at what time to look for the star. Then, about two minutes before the appointed time, he takes his place at the eyepiece. As he looks in he sees a number of vertical lines across his field of view. These are spider-threads placed in the focus of the eyepiece. Presently, as he looks, a bright point of silver light, often surrounded by little flashing, vibrating rays of colour, comes moving quickly, steadily onward — "swims into his ken", as the poet has it. The watcher's hand seeks the side of the telescope till his finger finds a little button, over which it poises itself to strike. On comes the star, "without haste, without rest", till it reaches one of the gleaming threads. Tap! The watcher's finger falls sharply on the button. Some three or four seconds later and the star has reached another "wire", as the spider-threads are commonly called. Tap! Again the button is struck.'

While spider-lines were helping astronomers with their measurements, the spiders themselves were still busy making their own sticky lines inside telescope tubes. The Newtonian telescope in particular, whose tube is open to the elements, was apparently notorious for attracting spiders and their webs, and a twenty-five feet long telescope in the Greenwich Observatory was such an attractive place for spiders that it finally had to be left to them. As an article in *Harper's* magazine reports, the telescope's 'cool and dark interior was so pleasant to the spiders that, do what they would, the astronomers could not altogether banish the persevering insects from it. Spin they would; and, spite of dusting and cleaning, and spider-killing, spin they did; and, at length, the savans [sic] got more instruments and less patience, and the spiders were left in quiet possession'. The astronomers apparently considered this as a case of poetic justice, in 'fair retaliation for the robberies the industrious insects had endured'. The problem and the spiders became larger when astronomers tried to create a worldwide star map in the late-nineteenth century. At the aptly named Prickly Point in Grenada, 'the richness of animal life proved a source of great annoyance... a dense spider's web was found... stretched across the slit of one of the spectroscopes'.

While astronomers mapped the stars, time was becoming a problem. For centuries, a sundial in each town had been used to regulate local time. This was accurate enough when travel within a country could take days, but with the invention of the railways journey times were reduced to just a few hours — and it was vital for this new transport that accurate timetables could be used throughout the country. One solution was to use a local meantime, which was measured not by a sundial but by the longitude of a location. This improved the accuracy of the measurement but didn't solve the problem: local times could differ from one station to the next by

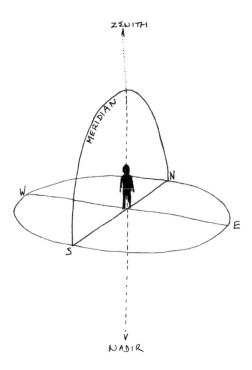

ZENITH

MERIDIAN

W

N

E

S

NADIR

up to 15 minutes. In Britain, 'Railway time' was eventually adopted, which used the Royal Observatory in Greenwich as the country's prime meridian, so that the time of the day was the same throughout the country.

A meridian is an imaginary line that arcs around the Earth. You can make your own. Wherever you are, look up. The point directly above you is called the 'zenith'. Imagine a line running north to south through the zenith — this is your (personal) meridian. If you fix a telescope where you stand, so that it can be moved in an arc along this imaginary line, then as the Earth rotates different stars will cross (or appear to cross) your meridian. Three things can now be measured in relation to each other: your position, the time, and the angle of the star above the horizon. If you had a map of stars, showing the angle at which they appear at a certain time and location, you could use this information to work out where you were.

Britain had standardised its time, but other countries had also adopted their own prime meridians. This created a further problem.

As European nations began to increase their land and wealth by colonising faraway countries, the ability to accurately locate and map ships and colonies was a vital tool in securing and sustaining power from a distance. An international standard time was needed to aid navigation across the oceans.

The 1884 International Meridian Conference was convened to decide upon a single prime meridian. Twenty-five nations were represented at the conference, and the majority voted to adopt the 'meridian passing through the centre of the transit instrument at the Observatory of Greenwich'.[3] This imaginary line that ran through the centre of the Airy Transit telescope would mark exactly 0° longitude. It would separate the sphere of the Earth into two halves: the eastern and western hemispheres. And at its centre, dividing east from west, was the silken thread of a female European garden spider. Her thread existed in neither hemisphere; it was perceived as an abstract line of measurement, lacking any physical presence. But the spider would have spun her pheromones into the thread of silk, telling any passing spider her age and reproductive history. And if a male spider had wandered into the Greenwich Observatory, he could have sniffed out these pheromones and made his way to the telescope. There, inside the eyepiece, he might have plucked at the thread of the prime meridian in a courtship serenade.

The use of spider lines seems an appropriate choice for a growing empire concerned with mapping and expansion. But this imaginative leap from seeing a spider web to using it as a straight line with which

3 Twenty-two of the nations represented at the conferences voted for the prime meridian to be set in Greenwich. San Domingo (now the Dominican Republic) voted against, while France and Brazil abstained. The French were concerned that an international meridian should be entirely neutral, and not be physically based in one country. The engineer Sandford Fleming, representing Canada, came up with the great idea of setting an 'anti-meridian' at Greenwich, so that zero degrees longitude would be set on the opposite side of the Earth in the middle of the Pacific ocean. In the end, however, in keeping with the majority of nautical charts of the time, Greenwich was adopted as the prime meridian — although France kept to its own 'Paris time' until 1911.

to measure requires a certain perspective. The prevalent western representation of a spider web is of a circle segmented by straight lines, but this is not the same everywhere. For example, the female mat weavers of the Yombe people of Southern Africa weave a pattern called *khondo-buba*, the 'spider's web', which depicts a series of interlocking repeating shapes in a symmetrical pattern. As the ethnomathematician Paulus Gerdes has described, 'When the people designate a village head as *khondo-buba*, this expresses the feeling of love they have for their headman, who has qualities of a spider that can catch the population in its web.' The spider's relation to its web mirrors the social structure of the village, a perception that is symbolised through the woven pattern. Similarly, the use of spider silk as a measurement tool in the West is not simply because it is a suitable material. Stretching back to antiquity, the spider web had been viewed as symbolic of the human position within the universe.

One of the earliest European sundials is thought to be the 'Arachne', the Greek word for spider. It was possibly created by the astronomer Eudoxus in the 4th century BC — quite a late development in comparison with the neighbouring cultures of Egypt and Mesopotamia, who by this point had been using sundials to measure time for over a thousand years. There is some debate over what the 'Arachne' sundial looked like, and how it was used, because it is not clear whether the term refers to the body of a spider, or its web. One possible Arachne sundial was unearthed in the 1980s among the remains of the temple of Amphiareion just outside Athens. It is a plane sundial, a flat stone semi-circle with twelve etched lines that run from the edge to the centre. This is where the gnomon is fixed — the name given to the object on a sundial that casts the shadow. The lines divided the daylight into twelve hours. As the sun appeared to move across the sky, the shadow of the gnomon would be cast onto the face of the sundial and mark the time. It was believed that the Earth was the fixed centre of rotating celestial spheres, one of which held the sun. The observer of the sundial would be standing at the centre of these spheres.

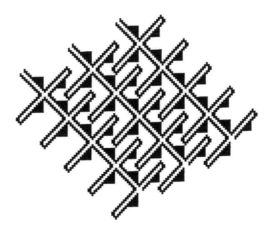

Khondo-buba, the 'spider web'
(courtesy of University of Washington Press)

Another possibility is that rather than being an actual object, 'Arachne' was the name given to a specific pattern. A spider web is formed of concentric circles and radiating lines, with a spider sitting in the centre. This so closely resembled the Classical conception of humans at the centre of celestial spheres, that the pattern is given the name Arachne — a word that encompasses both a spider's body and its web. The model of measurement is in perfect harmony with the structure of the universe.

How do you measure things that are inaccessible? As with the spider-lines in a telescope, you have to recreate it as a smaller, accessible model. Gnomons and their shadows have played an important role in this transformation. Thales, the Greek mathematician, used them to measure the height of one of the great pyramids. He sank a wooden peg into the sand in front of the pyramid and as the sun set, he measured the shadows cast by the pyramid and by the peg. Thales now knew the ratio of the peg to its shadow, and could apply the same ratio to measure the height of the pyramid.

In the eyepiece of a telescope, the spider silk lines are part of a similar miniaturised model. The lining-up of eye, eyepiece, spider silk, optical lens, and stars brings tangibility to the intangible; the world and the skies seem accessible. But with each step, further complexities reveal themselves.

Tony Kay is an engineer who runs his optical repair company from a workshop in a converted garage beside his bungalow in the seaside town of Selsey on the south coast of England. Broken binoculars, microscopes, telescopes and gun-sights are sent to him from across the world. He is one of the few remaining optical engineers to still use spider silk.

In his workshop, Tony shows me a small balsa wooden box containing nine numbered wooden frames, each secured within its numbered slot. He has written on the box in felt-tip pen, WEB STORE. The frames are almost identical to my own web collecting tools that I used on my walks — same form, same material. They are sized to fit the human hand and the spider's web. He collects silk in the garden behind the shed, 'you just sort of offer [the frame] up to the web, you hold it there and break it, and it just sticks to the wood'. The webs in his garden are small, he says, but if he visits somewhere with larger spiders, he will take his web store with him. He collects only a single thread, so that the spider can repair the gap without having to spin the entire web again. He then brings the silk into the workshop, and uses the threads to repair the broken crosshairs of gun sights. In modern manufacturing, the crossed lines that pinpoint the aim of the bullet are cast in one piece along with their circular surround; if one of the lines breaks, the entire eyepiece has to be replaced. Instead, Tony repairs the eyepiece by creating a new crosshair using the silk of spiders, which he says is finer than any wire available. And unlike metal wire, spider silk will not snap with the sudden recoil of a fired gun.

Tony Kay's use of silk follows a tale of the spider line that stretches back to a young German girl in New Jersey.

Just after the problem of time had been solved at the International Meridian Conference, Mary Pfeiffer arrived in Hoboken, New Jersey,

→ Tony Kay's web store

A broken reticule at Tony Kay's workshop

with her mother, brother and stepfather. She was one of hundreds of German immigrants who settled in Hoboken during this period, having come across the Atlantic on the Hamburg-America shipping line. In Hoboken was the factory of Keuffel and Esser that produced surveying and drafting instruments. At the age of fourteen, Pfeiffer went to work for them as the first full-time spider silk collector. There is no record of how the post was advertised, but Pfeiffer later said that it was her 'nimbleness of finger' that got her the job, and the fact that she was not afraid of spiders. She remained at the company for over fifty years, and it is possible that she was responsible for collecting the spider threads in the Smithsonian's micrometre.

Pfeiffer first appears in an article in the *New York Evening Mail*, just after the outbreak of the First World War. To avoid the anti-German sentiment that was spreading across the Atlantic, she had adopted the anglicised surname 'Piper'. It reported a worrying moment for

← One of Tony Kay's wooden frames, with a spider thread in the centre

the company: '200 spiders go on strike, but woman coaxes 'em back'. It seems that the spiders at Keuffel and Esser refused to produce silk, but Pfeiffer was able to get the spiders to spin again by tickling their toes and tapping their legs. Having worked at the company for twenty years, Pfeiffer now had her own spider team: a group of three girls who worked under her guidance in the basement of the factory. This was Pfeiffer's Spider Room. In the spring, a group of boys were employed to scour the marshes and barns of New Jersey for European garden spiders. These young spiders were taken to the spider room, where they roamed freely, filling the room with their webs.

As the names suggests, garden spiders prefer to live outdoors, and they require fresh prey. They would not have flourished in a sealed factory basement. To feed them, Pfeiffer would have had to put something in the room that attracted flies, such as fruit or meat. Rather than being a calm, quiet room of spinning spiders and young girls, the air was possibly filled with buzzing flies, webs and the stench of rotten food.

Surrounded by webs and flies, Pfeiffer would ask one of the girls to hold a spider in the flat of her hand and gently 'tickle' it. The spider would leap to the ground, creating a thread of silk running from its spinnerets to the girl. Pfeiffer would then approach with a wire coat hanger and slowly wind the silken strand, extracting several hundred feet of thread at a time.

To be able to collect reels of silk, it is important that the spider never touches the ground. If it does, it will immediately break off the thread by which it hangs and run away. Suspended by its safety-rope, it avoids breaking the silk thread, as it would fall. However, it still has the capacity to create new threads from its spinnerets. If these are caught by a gust of wind, and attach themselves to a nearby object, the spider will suddenly run along this thread, as if running through air, and break its attachment to the reel. The rhythm of collecting is important — it must be evenly paced and gentle. Holding the fork that it hangs from, you can feel the weight of the spider. Its legs dance in the air, attempting to find a hold. You tap the fork, the spider drops a little, and you reel in its silk. If the twisting of the fork is irregular or if it is done with too much vigour the spider will opt to break the thread with its back legs and fall

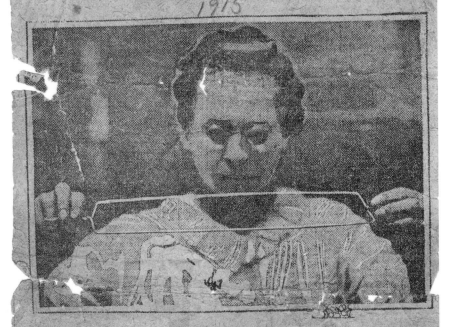

200 Spiders Go on Strike,
But Woman Coaxes 'Em Back

1915

Desperate Situation in Hoboken Plant When Insects That Furnish Cross Hairs for Surveying Instruments Refuse to Work—Again Spinning at Full Speed.

Mary Pfeiffer (*New York Evening Mail*, August 21, 1915)

to the ground. A few times, I have seen a spider produce what appears as a sheet of silk — thousands of threads at once from its spinnerets. It is sickeningly beautiful — like a rippling plane of transparent silver — but it is produced, no doubt, in a panic to escape.

Pfeiffer claimed that the spiders would occasionally suffer from bouts of melancholia, and would stop spinning. They must be humoured, she said, and given cheerful surroundings (it is not clear what 'cheerful surroundings' might be for a spider). A great deal is made in the newspaper article of the temper of the spiders and the girls who are able to work with them. Pfeiffer and her assistants are described as 'experts in the art of coaxing the spiders to produce and past masters of tactfulness. None but the most genial girls in the factory are selected for this work'. The description of 'genial' girls working with melancholic 'sleek fat fellows' makes them sound like the innocent handmaidens of a particularly repugnant and gloomy male master. The writer, however, is mistaken in his description of the sex of the spider — they were certainly all female.

The silk that Pfeiffer and her team collected was distributed to optical instrument makers across the country. Each of the reels of silk would be placed in boxes, stamped with the phrase 'CAUTION, Spider web on frame, handle with extreme care'. The threads were then attached within optical instruments and the eyepieces of surveyors' tools.

Twenty-five years later, just before she retired, Pfeiffer appeared again in an article in a women's magazine. 'To her, in large part, America owes the straightness of its roads, the trueness of its walls, and the accuracy of its scientific measurements.' Now that Pfeiffer is in her fifties, the writer cannot resist the image of a single woman, living alone and working with spiders. He describes Pfeiffer as 'a gray little woman in a print house dress' carrying on 'a strange partnership with a fat brown spider'. She 'looks like Whistler's mother'. She 'squints through steel rimmed "specs" and primly smooths the front of her dress as she talks.' She lives in 'a lonely four-room flat', its walls 'studded with religious pictures and symbols'. To the writer, Pfeiffer is in all senses a spinster — alone and spinning silk with her spinning spiders. There is no mention of the young girls or the tickling of feet.

Nan Songer in her sunroom with spiders (Nan Songer Hook, 'Spiders for Profit', *Natural History Magazine* (November 1955): 456–461.)

While Pfeiffer was nearing the end of her silk-collecting career, a woman on the other side of the United States realised the small-business potential of spider silk. During the Second World War there was a rise in demand for spider lines that could furnish both military surveying instruments and the telescopic sights of guns and periscopes. To fulfil this need, individuals across the United States began collecting spiders. One of the most successful was Nan Songer, who in 1939 established a 'spider farm' in her sunroom in California, where she kept 10,000 black widow spiders.

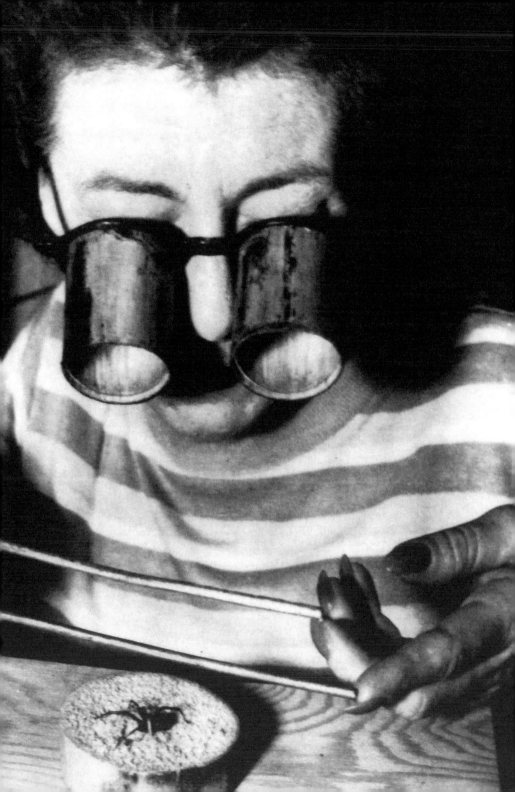

Rather than collecting silk by shaking or tickling the spider, Songer used a different process — one that took advantage of the spider's own technique of pulling silk from its body with its back legs. She fixed the spiders with a wire staple to a piece of cork. She then 'stroked' the spider's spinnerets and collected its silk onto a wooden frame. She too describes the importance of mood when collecting spider silk: the spider must be familiar with the person, and the room must be absolutely silent. Although black widow spiders are known for their poison, Songer describes them as 'docile as old milk cows'. The deadly spider becomes a domestic farmyard animal; it is 'silked' as cows are milked.

Songer would split the strands of silk with a needle. So that she was able to see the fine threads, she created a pair of magnifying glasses set in two hollow tubes made from the stalks of a yucca plant. She became so adept at collecting silk, and separating it into fine strands, that she was asked by the U.S. National Bureau of Standards to provide a standardised list of spider silk to specification. She produced a mail-order catalogue with silk ranging from 'extra fine' to 'extra heavy'. For particularly fine instruments, she also offered the silk of newly hatched spiders that measured 1/500,000th of an inch.

Contemporary newspaper and journal articles of the time declared that spiders were doing their bit for the war, and for business: 'Black widow spiders aid sharpshooters'; 'Spiders for national defence'; 'War-working spiders' and 'Spiders spin for war'. At the end of an article on Songer published in the *Los Angeles Times*, the journalist wrote: 'Because of Nan Songer... our gunners and bombardiers are able to draw a finer, more accurate sight on the enemies of the United States — wherever they are'. From lines that measured space and time, the spider lines became terrestrial — used by hunters to pinpoint the target of a bullet. A drawing that accompanies an article written by Nan Songer perhaps best illustrates this. Not only does it show the strange effects of scale in optical instruments, by which a spider can

← Nan Songer 'silking' a spider, while wearing magnifying glasses made from yucca plants (Nan Songer Hook, 'Spiders for Profit', *Natural History Magazine* (November 1955): 456–461.)

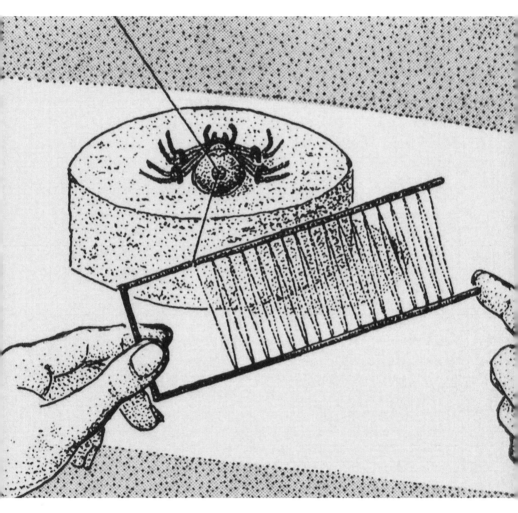

Silking spiders and splitting their threads (Illustration: George Childs. In Nan Songer Hook, 'Spiders for Profit', *Natural History Magazine* (November 1955): 456–461.)

'kill' a tiger, it also implies that the spider's own behaviour as a predator is in support of the killing of animals for pleasure. The spiders are apparently on our side, aiding the kill.

The demand for spider lines in optical instruments gradually declined, to be replaced by fine photographic printing methods, but its use persisted well into the late twentieth century. The lines of the Airy Transit telescope that once marked the Prime Meridian were still made of spider silk in the 1950s. One of the last people to take measurements with it was Gilbert Satterthwaite, who recalls: 'One of the chaps in the workshop used to regularly walk round the gardens [of Greenwich] looking for suitable webs — it was the long threads which anchored the web to bushes that were used. He had a wooden gadget rather like a catapult handle which he laid across the strand and then cut it either side, ending up with a dozen or so lengths. On his bench in the workshop he had a metal cabinet with a wooden frame inside to which he could transfer them. He liked to keep quite a number there, because at any time an observer might ring and ask for a broken wire to be replaced'.

At the Vickers' optical instrument factory in York, boys were still being sent out in the 1960s to look for spiders. They searched early in the morning, while the dew was still on the ground and on the spider webs, so that they were easier to spot. Each spider was placed in a separate pillbox to avoid them eating each other. Back at the factory, the silk would be collected in the same fashion as Pfeiffer used, on forks that each held four feet of web. Again, the importance of keeping the spider relaxed in this process is described: 'This operation requires some skill, as if the spider is unduly disturbed and becomes "hot and bothered" the web will be of irregular thickness'. After the silk had been collected, the spiders were returned to the common and new ones collected the next morning. The works manager at the factory, Eric Cussans, said in a company newsletter,

→ **A tiger in the crosshairs** (Nan Songer Hook, 'Spiders for Profit', *Natural History Magazine* (November 1955): 456–461.)

'We don't keep them long, as we shouldn't know how to feed them... They do us a good turn then we do them one by taking them back to their homes in the gorse'.

Back in his workshop in Selsey, Tony Kay tells me that he cannot remember when he thought of using spider silk for repairing broken gun sights, or if someone told him about the technique. It was simply the most suitable material for the job, and one that could extend the limited lifespan of modern tools. Knowledge about using spider silk is not necessarily passed down generations, rather it disappears and reappears when someone is looking for a material, and finds one close to hand. 'Spider's web', he says, 'you can't beat it'. Mounted on the wall behind him is a 'flying shuttle' — the tool that revolutionised the processes of weaving. He points at it, telling me it was invented by his ancestor, John Kay. It links the spider lines to a parallel tale of threads: the attempt to spin and weave with spider silk.

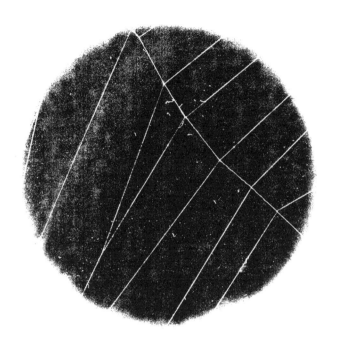

Weaving

The spiral is somebody who doesn't have a frame of reference. The only thing is this hanging, this fragility.
Louise Bourgeois

It is September and I'm walking through a clearing in a sandy forest looking for a particular spider. This is Folly Island, South Carolina. With a golf course at one end and a nature reserve at the other, Folly is a marshy sandbar slowly disappearing into the Atlantic Ocean. It is periodically rebuilt with dark sand pumped up from the depths of the sea and deposited along its shoreline. At 6am this morning I left the nearby city of Charleston and drove south along a single track, across the wooden bridge that joins Folly to the mainland, and for the past two hours I have been walking through the small patches of remaining forest — palms, sand, dead trees, bushes of berries I don't recognise, and darting lizards. I feel the panic of the spider hunter — not the fear of seeing spiders but the fear of missing them, of being too late in the season. Busy searching the bushes, and flapping away the mosquitoes, I am brought to a halt by what feels like a net pressed against my head. Looking up, my face is inches from a female *Nephila clavipes*, my hair entangled in the giant golden web she has spun across the path.

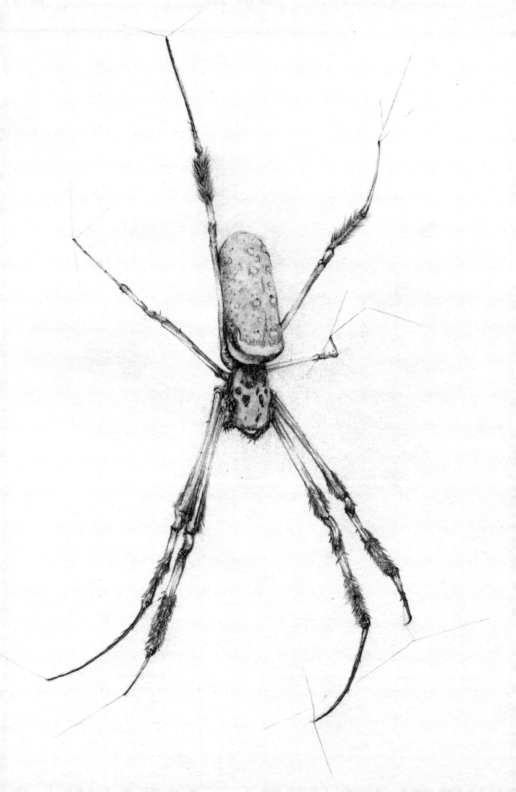

Weaving

In the clear morning light this spider is dazzling. The palm trees of Folly are not just green, they are glowing, in a pact with the sunlight, and the golden yellow silk of the *Nephila* dances between them. She sits in the centre of the web, and is so large that she must spin extra guy-ropes of threads behind the web to support her weight. Her body is long, thin and almost rectangular, light grey with a patterned yellow stripe down the centre. Her legs are striped dark red and black, with tufts of hair. She is about the size of my hand. She does not scurry, but moves slowly and deliberately. Carefully feeling, she stretches her fine front legs out before her and places them down on my skin.

Hanging in the corner of her web is a male. Like most other species of spider, the females are larger than the males, but in the case of the *Nephila* the size discrepancy is remarkable. The males are about a tenth of the size of the female, so that one or more might live on her web at any one time, feeding on the prey she captures and even mating with her without her seeming to respond or notice.

I am here on Folly Island to make a ring from her silk.

Folly Island was once more forest than beach. This changed when it became a key stronghold of the Union army during the American Civil War, from where they could attack the Confederate base of Charleston. In their letters home, the Union soldiers described the awful heat of summer on Folly, and the sickness and biting insects that flourished in its marshes. More died of disease than combat, and many suffered from boredom and homesickness. One soldier from Connecticut wrote 'the white sand, the monotonous moan of the surf at high and low tide, and the lifeless appearance of tree and shrub, all contribute to fill the mind of the soldier with despondence and gloom'. Soldiers passed the days of waiting on Folly by collecting shells on the beach, 'Day after day, at low tide, the whole beach, as far as eye could reach up and down, would be covered with men toiling as diligently... as if they were gathering diamonds'.

← *Nephila clavipes*   → Folly Island

Two soldiers, however, found a different way of passing the time. Dr Burt Green Wilder and Lieutenant Sigourney Wales were officers of the 55th Massachusetts regiment sent to Folly Island in 1863. Wilder was the regiment's assistant surgeon with a passion for zoology and comparative anatomy. The days between battles were his opportunity to explore the plants and creatures of Folly Island, many of which were unknown to him. It was on one of his meandering walks that he discovered a huge spider sitting in the centre of a golden web that stretched ten feet between the trees. Wilder collected the spider and put it in his hat to carry back to the camp. He held the hat in his teeth so that both his hands were free — one to break down the webs stretching across his path, the other to ward off mosquitoes. He made his way waist deep across the swamps. It was an unpleasant trip; 'What with the extreme heat and my previous fatigue, and the dread lest my captive should escape and revenge herself upon my face while I was avoiding the nets of her friends, and the relentless attacks of their smaller but more venomous associates, it was the most uncomfortable walk imaginable'. He returned to his tent in the camp, and took the spider in his hands; 'The insect was very quiet, and did not attempt to escape; but presently, after crawling slowly along my sleeve, she let herself down to the floor, taking first the precaution, after the prudent fashion of most spiders, to attach to the point she left a silken line, which, as she descended, came from her body. Rather than seize the insect itself, I caught the thread and pulled. The spider was not moved, but the line readily drew out, and, being wound upon my hands, seemed so strong that I attached the end to a little quill, and, having placed the spider upon the side of the tent, lay down on my couch and turned the quill between my fingers'. He continued at this for an hour and a half, after which time he had collected over one hundred and fifty yards of 'the most brilliant and beautiful golden silk I had ever seen'.

Meanwhile, during lookout duty, Sigourney Wales had also come across this spider and its golden coloured silk. He had been spending his free time carving metal trinkets and medals, but on discovery of

→ **Spider silk spinning machine patent**, Burt Wilder and Sigourney Wales, January 9, 1866

Wilder, Wales & Nichols.
Mode of Producing Silk from Insects.
Nº 51,988. Patented Jan. 9, 1866.

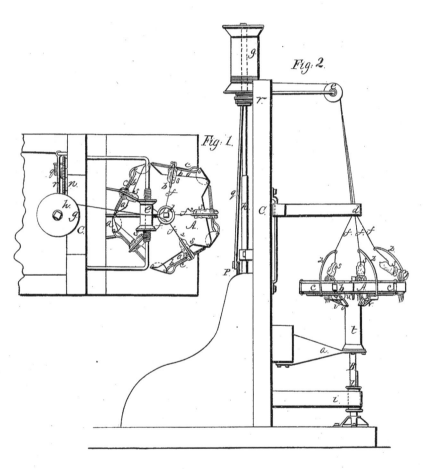

Fig. 2.

Fig. 1.

Witnesses:

A. S. Hale Jr.

G. H. Washburn

Inventors:

B. G. Wilder, S. Wales and William Nichols

By their Attorney.

H. H. Ludy

Wilder, Wales & Nichols.
Mode of Producing Silk from Insects.

Nº 51,988.   Patented Jan. 9, 1866.

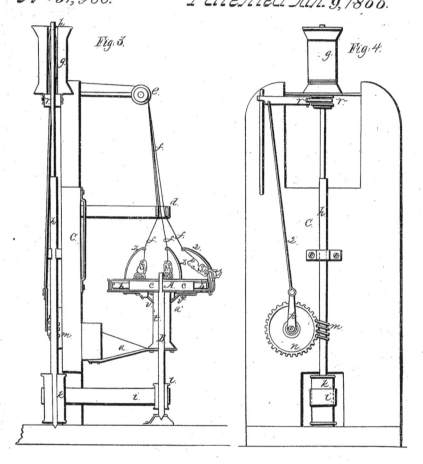

Fig. 3.   Fig. 4.

Witnesses: Inventors:

O. P. Hale Jr.   B. G. Wilder, S. Wales and William Nichols
G. H. Washburn   by their attorney.
                               R. H. Eddy.

the spider he had found another potential material. Using a spool with rubber rings attached, he wound the silk directly from the spider's spinnerets to create a series of golden rings. These he was apparently able to sell as real gold jewellery to the other soldiers in his regiment.

Wilder and Wales discovered their mutual interest in the local spider, and became convinced of the commercial potential of its golden silk. Once the war had ended, Wilder wrote that he believed that the silking of the large *Nephila* spiders of the southern states could offer an occupation for the freed slaves, but that it required the invention of some kind of tool that could twist together the thin silken threads into a strand that was thick enough to be woven into cloth. Along with Wilder's father-in-law, the men submitted a patent for a spider silk spinning machine.

> *51,988 — Mode of Obtaining Silk from Living Spiders and Other Silk*
>   *First, We claim the drawing and reeling or winding the silk directly from the insect, spider, silk worm, or other silk producers, as set forth.*
>   *Second, We claim the drawing, reeling and spinning or turoting [sic] together directly from the bodies of insects, spiders, silk worms, or other silk producers, two or more strands or threads, as set forth.*

The drawings that accompany the patent reveal a torturous machine. The spiders are held upside down on a rotating disk and their legs and bodies are strapped to prevent them cutting their silk with their back legs. As the disk was turned, the silk from each spider was drawn upwards and twisted into a thicker strand. From these threads, Wilder was able to weave a small ribbon of golden silk. However, spiders are difficult to keep — not only do they need a continuous supply of live prey, they also have a tendency to eat each other. Added to these problems was the vast amount of time it took to collect even a small amount of silk. Eventually, the men gave up their attempts to develop a spider silk industry. Wilder became professor of zoology at Cornell University, where, by his own bequest, his brain is preserved in the university collection, while Wales became a travelling salesman.

The history of humans attempting to weave with spider silk is scattered with similar tales: optimistic belief in the commercial possibilities of spiders, followed by realisation of the difficultly of the task. Yet there's something about the resemblance of spider silk to thin threads of precious metals that has repeatedly attracted western inventors. As Wilder describes, 'Perhaps its greatest, and certainly its most obvious advantage over all other known fabrics, is one which it is impossible to represent, and which even words fail to describe; its peculiar and exceeding beauty. If you can picture to yourself a mass of pure and yellow gold, which not only reflects the light as from a smooth and polished surface, but which has all the depth and softness of liquid amber, you may realise in some degree the wonderful appearance of a sheet of spiders' silk as seen in the sunshine; and even in the shade its lustre is greater than that of gold'. To weave with gold — to create fabrics that shimmered like precious metals. This was the dream of the spider silk weavers.

Standing in the scrubland of Folly Island, I have my wooden spool ready to reel the silk and create a golden ring, but I've lost the spider. It was here a moment ago, when I went to set up my video camera, but it's now disappeared and I am feeling guilty, because I had moved her from her web to where the light was better for filming. I was planning to return her, but now she's somewhere on the sandy ground. How do you find a spider in a forest? It's hot, but I'm wearing long sleeves and trousers to stop the flies biting. Looking through the trees to the beach beyond I can see people sunbathing. There is a slight touch on my wrist, a caress. I look down. The spider has been crawling over my body the entire time.

The story of weaving with spider silk begins in southern France in the early eighteenth century. François Xavier Bon de Saint Hilaire, a magistrate in the city of Montpellier, decided to investigate the potential of a spider silk industry that could compete with that of the silkworm.

Spiders, he believed, had been unfairly ignored as possible producers of silk threads because of the public's general dislike of these animals. 'Spiders make a Silk, as beautiful, strong and glossy, as common Silk: The prejudice that is entertained against so common and despicable an Insect, is the reason why the Publick has been hitherto ignorant of the Usefulness of it.' On examining the spiders in his garden, Bon divided them into two types: those that have long legs, and those that have short legs. It is, he says, the ones with short legs that provide the best silk, and it is the males rather than the females. However, he had incorrectly identified the female — her epigyne tends to protrude from her body, which Bon assumed was indicative of a male.

Bon's knowledge of working with silk was taken from sericulture, in which silkworm cocoons are boiled and the threads extracted. He used a similar technique on the spiders and collected and boiled their nests. 'I beat [the spider silk] well for some time with the Hand and a

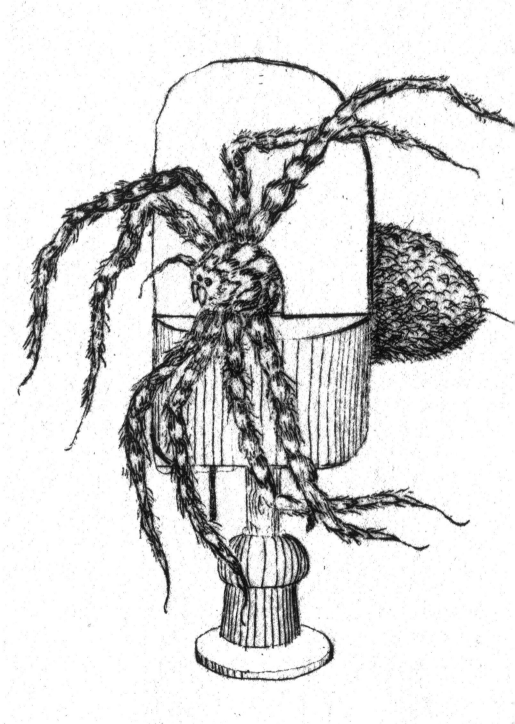

Termeyer's spider spinning machine

small Stick, to free them from Dust. Then I washed them in warm Water, 'till the Water that came from them was clear. After this, I let them steep in a large Pot, with Soap, Saltpetre, and some pieces of Gum-Arabick; and let the whole boyle 2 or 3 hours over a gentle Fire. Then I washed them again with warm Water, to free them from the Soap'. After boiling and carding the spider silk, he then wove the threads on a knitting-frame. He created three pairs of spider silk stockings, two of which he presented to the Académie Royale des Sciences in Paris and the third to Sir Hans Sloane at the Royal Society in London. Bon's hope was that these silk stockings would gain him membership of these illustrious clubs.

Their response was not positive. The Académie Royale did ask one of their members, the prolific scientist René Antoine de Réaumur, to investigate Bon's work, but his conclusion was that spider silk weaving had no potential as a commercially profitable activity. He listed three limiting factors. The first was the difficulty of collecting and housing the spiders — particularly the problem of trying to prevent the spiders from eating each other. The second was supplying the animals with fresh prey, and the last was the inferior quality and yield of spider silk compared to that of the silkworm.

I can find no trace of Bon's spider stockings. They may have disappeared or been mistaken for silkworm stockings (the two materials appear very similar without the aid of a microscope). Bon's more lasting legacy is the term 'spider silk'. The analogous relationship between spiders spinning and a weaver's web was transformed into a potential material for human production.

Bon's belief that spiders could potentially replace silkworms is caricatured in Jonathan Swift's *Gulliver's Travels*. Gulliver visits the Grand Academy of Lagado, in which he finds men occupied with harnessing the activities of spiders, and attempting to alter the colour of their webs by changing their diet. 'I went into another room, where the walls and ceiling were all hung round with cobwebs, except a narrow passage for the artist to go in and out. At my entrance, he called aloud to me, "not to disturb his webs". He lamented "the fatal mistake the world had been so long in, of using silkworms, while we had such plenty of domestic insects who infinitely excelled the former, because they understood how to weave, as well as spin"'.

Forty years after the publication of *Gulliver's Travels*, a Spanish Jesuit priest would live in just such a room. Abbé Ramon de Termeyer was a missionary and amateur naturalist. His varied research included experiments on electric eels, a proposal for an antidote to viper venom and a short paper on how to keep eggs fresh during long journeys. He also had an interest in spiders. His house in Milan was filled with thousands of them, suspended from separate canes all around the house. They were fed by a steady supply of flies that bred in the piles of rotten meat that Termeyer had put out for them.

Termeyer extracted silk from the spiders' cocoons, with which his cousin Lucrezia Rasponi knitted a pair of silk stockings for King Charles III of Spain. These spider stockings have also since disappeared. Termeyer found that silk from spider cocoons was difficult to work with because not much could be gathered at a time, so he experimented with extracting silk directly from the spider. He designed a machine on which the spider was pinned to a piece of cork, with its legs on one side, and its spinnerets on the other. This prevented the spider from being able to cut the silken thread with its back legs, which meant that its silk could be continuously drawn out onto a spool.

Termeyer described the silk he collected as appearing like a mirror, or polished metal — and far superior in its brilliance and beauty to that of the silkworm. He was convinced of its commercial possibility. He had solved the problems that Réaumur had listed — he kept his spiders on separate canes so they could not eat each other; they had a steady supply of food which was easy to provide and he had discovered that the silk they produced on his machine was stronger and more vibrant than that of the silkworm. He suggested that many spiders could be attached to a machine in this way, and their silk reeled and twisted together. In spite of Termeyer's enthusiasm, his machine for twisting together the strands of silk directly from spiders was never realised. Yet it bears remarkable resemblance to the machine devised by Wilder and Wales in the United States over a century later.

People can extract silk from spiders without realising it. The tiny money spiders that often run across your hands and clothes are fun to play with. As a child, I would dangle them and with a slight shake of my hand the spider would drop, letting out a little more of its thread. Then, I'd catch it with my other hand and dangle again. Money spiders are small, and I would soon let them run away. Golden orb spiders are huge. They cannot be dangled and their silk is not a wisp of gossamer. To collect a single strand of silk from their webs you have to tug it, cut it, or bite it with your teeth.

In the early days of spider silk weaving the spider most often used was the garden spider, as this was the most visible and available to Europeans.[4] But by the nineteenth century, with the craze for colonial exploration and collection, tropical spiders and their webs reinvigorated the dream of establishing a spider silk industry. European travellers in South America and the West Indies sent home reports of large spiders and their industrial potential as giant silk producers. The webs of these spiders were reportedly so large and strong that they could capture birds or the hat of a passing explorer. One English traveller in Brazil wrote, 'The spider's web, which, in single threads, could support a straw hat, must be much stronger and tougher than the frail tissues of our own country, and might certainly be manufactured into articles of wearing apparel, if a proper quantity of it could be obtained'.

European travellers were surprised not only by the large size of the spiders' bodies and webs, but also by the vast number of spiders that gathered together. Charles Darwin recounted in his 1839 journal of the

---

4 One such example is a Londoner Daniel Rolt, who in 1830 was living in Friday Street near St Paul's Cathedral where he was struck by 'reflection of the light on the immacuable [sic] webs' in his garden. He decided to collect its silk by attaching its thread to a steam engine, which he had borrowed from the factory in which he worked. For this, he won a silver medal from the Royal Society of Arts — but like the Académie Royale over a century before, they were unconvinced of its commercial potential.

Photograph of Malagasy women in the late nineteenth century employed at the spider farm to look after the *Nephila* spiders. (Courtesy Musée des Confluences, Lyon)

voyage of the Beagle that the number of spiders in Brazil 'in proportion to other insects, is here compared with England very much larger'. There are so many of them, he wrote, that 'every path in the forest is barricaded with the strong yellow web of a species'.

Samples of these tropical silks were sent to Europe from across the world to be assessed. The Royal Botanical Gardens in Kew received a bundle of spider silk from their representative in India, with the message 'I believe if it can be obtained in quantity it might be packed in bales and sent to England, where it would readily find a market for being carded and spun into spun silk for sewing or weaving purposes'.

Meanwhile, in the Madagascan capital of Antananarivo, the French colonial government took things further, with the creation of a spider farm in the newly established technical college in the capital.

They employed Malagasy women as spider hunters, responsible for collecting the *Nephila* spiders and rehousing them on bamboo canes erected around the college. Under the direction of a M. Nogué, they placed each spider in a vice which bound its legs. The silk was extracted and twisted together to form a thread which could be woven. There is some suggestion in contemporary reports that before the arrival of the French there was already a Malagasy custom of using spider threads to attach flowers to sunshades. M. Nogué had a grander aim: to create a woven spider silk fabric to display at the 1900 Paris *Exposition Universelle*. These colonial exhibitions were designed to celebrate the achievements of the colonies and, by extension, the power of the nations that ruled them. No one had attempted to weave spider silk on such a large scale.

After four years of spinning and weaving, M. Nogué sent to Paris a bed adorned with a canopy of golden spider silk. 'The dream of making silk from the threads spun by spiders has been made a reality', declared one newspaper report. Once it went on display, it was described in glowing terms: 'The cloth of spider silk recalls the robes of Sleeping Beauty. It has a wonderful brilliance and its iridescence sends the rays of the rainbow to astonished eyes. The silk of the spider is a superb golden yellow with reflections that are varied and dazzling.'

As befits such a fairytale object, the cloth disappeared after the exhibition closed and it has never been found. An article written just before the bed hangings were displayed suggests what might have happened: 'One of the new materials to be shown at the Paris Exhibition is the "spiders' silk". It is made from the webs of the large Madagascar spider, and is pale gold in colour. It is not suitable for dresses, for there is no wear in it, but will be made up into ties, cravats, ruchings, or any of those smaller articles of the toilet that are not expected to be anything but ephemeral'. Without a microscope these ephemeral articles would look like silkworm silk. The spider bed hanging may still exist as fine golden trims on antique Victorian clothing.

→ Two women spinning spider silk (courtesy Musée des Confluences, Lyon, France. Image credit L. Sonthonnax.)

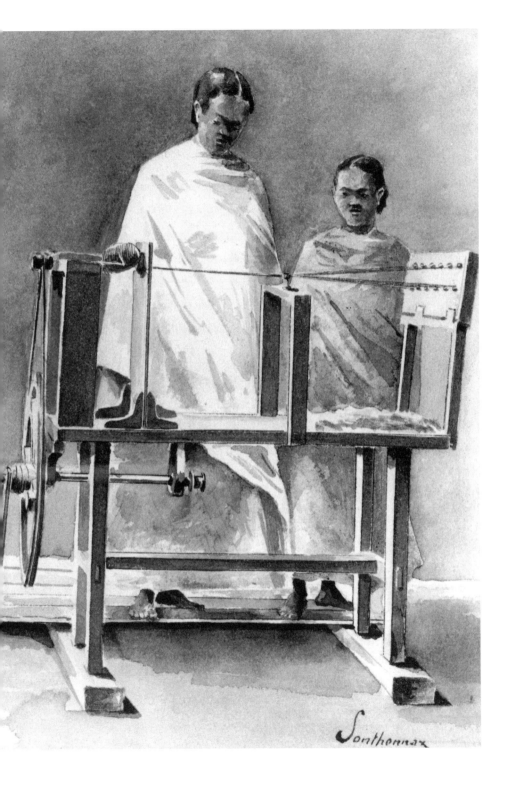

Sonthonnax

I have made a spool out of some bits of wood and the handle of a broken drill. At the centre I have secured, with Blu-tack, a black metal ring onto which I'm going to wind the threads of golden spider silk. Initially, I wanted to do everything right — to entirely reconstruct the contraption on which Sigourney Wales might have made his spider silk jewellery on Folly Island. He would, I think, have used whatever was to hand for a soldier on the island — I'm imagining bullets, metal boxes, leather, twine, and shells. I spend a lot of time looking at bits of Civil War memorabilia in the museum in Charleston. These are prized, valuable objects, not things I can borrow for a spider re-enactment. I become completely distracted by local Civil War history: the sea fort designed in the shape of a baseball pitch (or perhaps it was the other way round) and the first successful use of a submarine in battle — described as such because it hit its target, yet all the soldiers inside the submarine were trapped and drowned. I try to connect this to spiders, to the spider line in the eyepiece of a periscope, or the web-like shape of a radar display in a submarine. The trouble with working with threads is that they can connect anything.

During the nineteenth century the growing interest in spiders and their silks was not only because of their commercial potential. While the spiders on the farm in Madagascar were spinning their threads, a story began to circulate in Europe and America of the Mughal Emperor Aurengzeb who was forced to reprove his daughter for 'the indelicacy of her costume, although she wore as many as seven thicknesses of spider cloth'. It is not clear where this story originated, it perhaps stemmed from the contemporary fashion for veil dances which nurtured western fantasies of oriental harems. Even more delicate than silkworm silk, these are gossamer threads — at once concealing and revealing.

While the story of the Mughal Emperor's daughter was being told and retold, a fabric called 'spider web' became fashionable among wealthy women in London and Paris. Rather than being made of spider

silk, this was silkworm silk that had been woven with a 'spider web fineness'.[5] These dainty threads worked to entice and obscure the gaze of an onlooker. In 1891, a regular column on women's fashion reported that nets and trimmings for underskirts should be made of 'spider web', 'so that a little switch of the upper skirt may reveal the lovely underskirt with its coquettish frou frou flounces'. Later articles advise that 'spider web' should be used as veils on women's hats, thereby 'veiling the beautiful' with a 'network of silk'.

The use of fine silk to reveal and conceal women's bodies becomes prevalent during this period, particularly as a material to create lingerie

---

5 The name for this cloth is particularly confusing, as its popularity coincides with newspaper articles claiming that a spider silk industry has been established in Madagascar. These become conflated, so that a 1907 article in *The Washington Post* describes spider factories in Madagascar, where 'beautiful silken fabrics' are woven to be 'shipped to Paris and made up into ladies' gowns'. It seems very unlikely that spider silk was ever made into dresses as there are no extant examples and such an endeavour would have taken years of work simply to make one dress.

for the fast growing middle-class market. This was accompanied by magazine advice columns explaining when and how women should wear such private garments. One article described the charms of the 'conjugal chemise':

'Do not describe it to young girls — one must respect the exquisite and somewhat excessive modesty of the seraphim — but it must be placed in their bridal trousseau. They will not wear it immediately; but after a while they will understand the value of this oriental silk or batiste, with large lace inserts, all aquiver with valenciennes flounces that embellish it at the hem. They will become accustomed to this transparent network, which in front — from the beginning of the bosom to the belt — reveals the charming graces of a young and supple bust'.

These gossamer fabrics made of transparent networks are the robes of young brides, who must both know and not know its enticing effects. Its erotic potential is in this hovering moment — she must be innocent and awakening to experience, just as the fabric at once conceals and reveals her 'charming graces'. Like the daughter of the Mughal Emperor, no matter how many layers of gossamer she wears, she will still be naked.

The possible effects of these new gossamer fabrics are described in a contemporary passage written by the French historian and critic Hippolyte Tain, in which a middle-aged bachelor (a thinly disguised Tain) describes the men and women of Parisian high society. In the following extract, he has been watching a girl of sixteen each night as she attends the opera with her family. She wears a 'close-fitting' dress of silk that shows her figure, and around her chest is a 'soft nest of lace'. He writes:

'She is still too young to suspect the exact effect of her toilette; her ideas are too vague and too new; it is I who at this moment am explaining this effect as a sculptor, as a man of the world; she would blush to hear my explanation — and yet, in the half daylight of her thoughts, she has some suspicion of it... she half sees, in a diaphanous and golden mist, a whole aurora of things. A very rose asleep while the vapors of morning are vanishing, and masses of luminous whiteness are spreading over the pearly sky, she listens, motionless and as in a dream, to the beatings of distant wings, the indistinct rustle of a whole world of insects which will soon come buzzing and murmuring around her heart'.

As with the young bride wearing her conjugal chemise, the girl is held in a state between innocence and knowledge. But in Tain's description, she is also motionless, and waits, listening to the approaching 'insects' that are drawn to her. This is an extraordinary metaphor — she is not like a candlelight drawing moths, as candles do not listen; rather, Tain seems to be comparing her to a spider enticing insects into its web. As she awakens from girlish innocence, she draws buzzing and murmuring men to her silken heart.

Until recently only a few samples of woven spider silk existed as evidence of the colonial spider silk industry in Madagascar. The quai Branly museum in Paris has in its collection a ten centimetre square piece of golden ribbon with silk tassels mounted on board, while the Musée des Confluences in Lyon has a collection of bobbins of spider silk (see colour insert: Fig 3 and 4).[6]

Woven spider silk and its seductive qualities might have remained a Victorian fantasy. But a decade ago Simon Peers, an English textile manufacturer and historian based in Madagascar, discovered the story of the colonial spider farm and began the task of recreating it in his own 'spidery'. Working with his business partner Nicholas Godley and a team of Malagasy weavers and embroiderers they collected the silk of millions of native golden orb spiders, *Nephila madagascariensis*. During the spider spinning months of summer and autumn there was a daily routine. Starting early in the morning between sixty to eighty people would scour the area around Antananarivo for golden orb spiders in bushes and telegraph poles where they had woven their huge webs. The spiders were collected in boxes and taken to the spidery, where twenty-four were placed inside individual holders with their legs strapped down. Silk was pulled from each individual spider, and threaded through a single ring. On the other side of these rings, the threads were twisted together and wound onto cones. This silking

---

6 Lyon was for centuries the centre of French sericulture, and M. Nogué probably sent the samples of spider silk there in the hope that the French silk manufacturers would support his endeavours in the colonies.

process took about twenty-five minutes, until between 30 and 50 metres of thread were collected. The spiders were then returned outside at the end of the day. As with the spider collecting women of M. Nogué's spider farm, Malagasy women were responsible for the task of silking the spiders. In a separate room, the silk was twisted with another to create strands thick enough for loom weaving.

In 2012, after eight years of spinning and weaving spider silk, Peers and Godley exhibited two pieces at the Victoria and Albert Museum in London. One was a lamba akotifahana, a traditional Malagasy woven cloth that measured 11 feet by 4 feet. But the centrepiece of the exhibition was a golden spider silk cape, gleaming under spotlights inside a large glass case and embroidered with images of spiders (see colour insert: Fig 5).

Rather than a transparent network of gossamer threads, the golden cape looked heavy and thick, like a priest's robe. And yet it was made of a material that feels, literally, of nothing. When I met with Peers he placed a few threads of *Nephila* silk on my hand. It was golden bright, but if I closed my eyes I could not feel it.

The golden silk cape first appeared to the public in newspaper images and television reports during the weeks leading up to the exhibition. Worn by a model, and photographed in the Victoria and Albert galleries, these images illustrated a tantalising possibility that few would experience — that of wearing or even touching the cape. The female model in the photographs seemed as static in her pose as the young Parisian girl who in her silken dress 'listens, motionless and as in a dream, to the beatings of distant wings'. To weave with such a material was to achieve something seemingly impossible — the cape was an object more suited to fairy tales and dreams than material reality. As Peers and Godley described, their desire was to make something impermanent, permanent: to fix the ephemeral web into a lasting work of art.

When it weaves its web, a *Nephila* spider changes the colour of its silk depending on the environment. In shady areas, the web will be silver or a very pale yellow, while in sunlight the spider will spin a bright yellow-orange silk. It seems that these threads of silvery gold are particularly attractive to passing insects, as they associate the colour with their food source of yellow and white flowers. The woven cape exhibited at the Victoria and Albert museum is not a uniform gold, but varies from a pale silvery yellow to a bright yellow gold. Fixed within the cape these differing colours tell something of the space and time in which the object was created. It acts as a map and a narrative of the changing light over three years — the lighter gold perhaps tracing the overcast days, while the bright yellow threads mark the days when the sunlight filled the room. There are also slightly pinkish tinges within the cape. Peers told me that during a particularly hot summer, the hands of the embroiderers began to sweat as they worked on the cape, and the sweat turned the silk pink. The colour of the cape — from light yellow, to orange gold, to pink — traces the relationship between the makers, the material and the environment in which it was formed. These subtleties, less noticeable than the embroidered images of spiders, tie the making of the object to a particular body and moment. The cape is like a weather map.

The magic and value of the golden cape lies in the material of spider silk — in the impossibility of creating such an object, and the fantasies of entrapment and seduction that are associated with the material. To weave, one must extract only the dry silk from the spider, eliminating the sticky silk, the shape of a spider web, bits of fly, and the spider itself. Yet these are the visual clues that tell us that the material is spider silk — without them, the material appears simply as normal silk. So the spider is put back into the material through illustration — the cape is covered in embroidered representations of spiders.

There is something awkward about the need to remove and then reinstate the role of spiders in making these objects. In my own work, I began with collecting only the dry silk of spiders for weaving or drawing — I discarded the stickiness and the dust. Woven cloth is dry, unbroken and, ideally, permanent. To weave with spider silk exhibits a strange unease between the continuous activities of the spider/spinner and what we want the material to do — to glow forever like precious metal, with delicate fineness. It is this unease that I believe is at the heart of a Classical tale of a weaving girl who was turned into an endlessly spinning spider.

In his *Metamorphoses* Ovid tells the tale of a humble Lydian girl named Arachne. Her mother is dead, while she and her father are 'ordinary'. There is one thing that makes her exceptional, and that is her skill at weaving. The nymphs of the waters and earth gather around to watch her work. Ovid describes in tangible detail this process of making; a movement of hands and threads: 'she was winding the rough yarn into a new ball, or working the stuff with her fingers, teasing out the clouds of wool, repeatedly, drawing them into long equal threads, twirling the slender spindle with practised thumb, or embroidering with her needle'. You could tell, he says, that she had learned her skills from the goddess Athene. But Arachne says that she has no teacher and challenges Athene to a weaving contest.

Athene appears disguised as an old woman, telling Arachne to ask for the goddess's forgiveness for her rash and arrogant claims. Arachne refuses, calling the disguised Athene 'Weak-minded and worn out by tedious old age'. It is then that the goddess reveals herself, and Arachne must contest. She 'rushes on to her fate, eager for a worthless prize'. Both position themselves at their looms, and here again Ovid pauses in the drama to detail the technical process: 'The frame is fastened to the cross-beam; the threads of the warp separated with the reed; the thread of the weft is inserted between, in the pointed shuttles that their fingers have readied; and, drawn through the warp, the threads of the weft are beaten into place, struck by the comb's notched teeth'. The two 'work quickly, and, with their clothes gathered in tight, under their breasts, apply skilful arms, their zeal not making it seem like work'. Arms move with threads and the thick rustle of women's clothes, gathered out of the way for working.

Athene weaves a tapestry depicting the twelve gods of Athens 'in majesty' on their thrones. She weaves herself armed with shield, spear and helmet, and the other gods with their 'familiar attributes'. In the four corners of the tapestry, she weaves a scene to teach Arachne a lesson. Each shows mortals being punished by the gods for their arrogance. Around the tapestry she weaves a border made from the olive wreaths of peace, her own tree. Athene's tapestry is one of rule and order, both in its subject and its symmetrical appearance.

Arachne then replies. She weaves the lives of mortals deceived by the shape-shifting gods. Ovid describes a living tapestry; Arachne does not illustrate Jupiter in the form of a bull, while he deceives Europa, rather, 'you would have thought it a real bull'. Arachne goes beyond the borders of the object to make something that is itself alive and around the edge are 'flowers interwoven with entangled ivy' — a wild garden, in contrast to Athene's border of olive wreaths. Arachne's tapestry, writes Ovid, was faultless.

'Neither Pallas [Athene] nor Envy itself could fault that work. The golden-haired warrior goddess was grieved by its success, and tore the tapestry, embroidered with the gods' crimes, and as she held her shuttle made of boxwood from Mount Cytorus, she struck Idmonian Arachne, three or four times, on the forehead. The unfortunate girl could not bear it, and courageously slipped a noose around her neck: Pallas, in pity, lifted her, as she hung there, and said these words, "Live on then, and yet hang, condemned one, but, lest you are careless in future, this same condition is declared, in punishment, against your descendants, to the last generation!" Departing after saying this, she sprinkled her with the juice of Hecate's herb, and immediately at the touch of this dark poison, Arachne's hair fell out. With it went her nose and ears, her head shrank to the smallest size, and her whole body became tiny. Her slender fingers stuck to her sides as legs, the rest is belly, from which she still spins a thread, and, as a spider, weaves her ancient web.'

The transformation of Arachne into a spider is not carried out because of anger, but because of compassion. It is Athene's fury that leads her to strike Arachne, who would rather hang herself than endure such punishment, but it is Athene's pity at such a sight that causes her to change Arachne into a spider. She will hang, spin and weave forever in the body of a spider, as will her descendants, because

of her transgression against the superiority of the gods. But, she will live. Ovid finishes by telling us that the tale of Arachne spreads through the towns and 'fills the whole world with talk'. The story transforms into gossip, tales and murmurings, while Arachne and her descendants weave their webs.

The story of Arachne has been used over the centuries as a moral lesson of the dangers of transgressing the correct order of things. The earliest extant representation of the tale of Arachne is a relief of Athene/ Minerva striking Arachne on the walls of the Forum Transitorium in Rome. Built by the Emperor Domitian in the first century AD, it was intended as a moral guide, and a warning to women not to transgress the social laws of appropriate female behaviour. But a myth is not a moral lesson or a guide to follow; it is a shifting thing that may be transformed by another teller.

There is one figure in the story that tends to be treated as an unquestionably awful creature: the spider. It is not simply its appearance. Arachne's punishment is that she will be forever in a state of making — without the completion of an object. While the continuous making of webs is essential to a spider's life cycle, for a culture that values the fixed and completed object, it is horrific.

Weaving

On Folly Island, I am failing to recreate the ring. I can't draw silk directly from the golden orb spiders because I find them too large. They are alive, responsive, and I can see their eyes. Instead, I look for any webs that the spiders have deserted, and wind these onto my metal ring. It's difficult to prise the silk threads from their supports, to avoid bringing with them all the bits of leaf and twig to which they are attached. You cannot break these webs easily and I have no knife. I go at them with my mouth and teeth.

Layering

We are drawn into the pattern and held inside it, impaled,
as it were, on its bristling hooks and spines.
Alfred Gell

In front of me is a 'smothering hood'. One metre in length and cone-shaped, it is formed entirely from spider webs. Its colour is yellowy brown, but on closer inspection I can see layers of entangled threads, each a slightly different shade. And in these threads appear tiny fragments: bits of dust, splinters of wood, and the single leg of a long-dead insect. It is light in weight, and drapes across my arms as I hold it. I must wear gloves when handling museum objects, but I roll up my sleeve and put the inside of my bare wrist against the cloth. It feels soft, but with the scratch of captured bodies poking through.

The pharmaceutical entrepreneur and collector Henry Wellcome bought the smothering hood at a London auction in 1928 from a 'Mr Webb'. It cost six pounds fifteen shillings, equivalent to £400 today, and was later donated to the Science Museum in London. It was made in Malakula, the second largest island of the Republic of Vanuatu, an archipelago in the South Pacific, once known by its colonial title, the New Hebrides. According to the Museum's records,

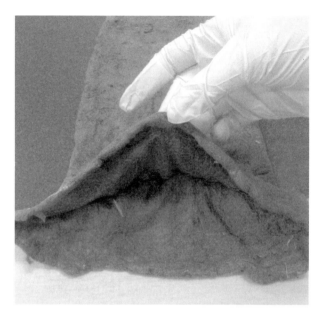

Inside the 'smothering hood'
(Inv. A173615 Science Museum, London)

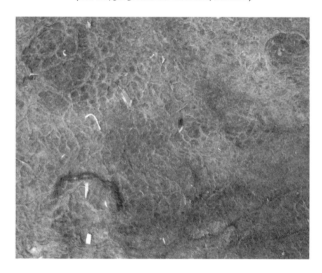

Close up of the 'smothering hood'

the smothering hood was used to suffocate widows immediately after the death of their husbands, so that they might continue their 'wifely ministrations' in the next world. Similar hoods from Vanuatu are found in the collections of other British museums. In the Pitt Rivers museum in Oxford, a spider web hood is labelled 'cap of death', and is reported to be used to cover a widow's face while she was strangled at her husband's funeral. Two similar hoods in the storage rooms of the British Museum have more whimsical definitions — one is described as a 'night cap' worn by the people of Vanuatu to keep their heads warm while they sleep, while the other is tentatively labelled 'a (smoking?) cap'. A London missionary based in Samoa at the end of the nineteenth century wrote in his letters home that rather than being a hood to keep the head warm, or a method of killing widows, these hoods were placed 'loaded with spiders' over the heads of criminals. In addition to these varied descriptions, there is some confusion among the collectors about how these spider web hoods were created; some contemporary commentators write that the people of Vanuatu made the hoods, others believe they are created entirely by spiders, while the notes accompanying the 'nightcap' in the British Museum claim that it is the collaborative effort of humans and spiders: 'The people make a slight framework & leave it in some dark spidery corner & eventually this is spun'.

All these hoods — the smothering hood, the cap of death, the nightcap and the smoking cap — have been mislabelled. The actual creation and use of these objects is tied to the cycle of life and death, but in a very different way to that described in the museum catalogues. Unlike the technique of weaving with spider silk, these spider web hoods make use of the material's own method of attachment: stickiness. Everything that is stuck to the web is invited: a fly's wing, a leaf, and perhaps the spider itself.

Most spider web fabric is made in the southwest region of Malakula. Linguistically and culturally it is one of the most diverse islands in the world. As with many other Oceanic cultures, Malakula has no tradition

A NIGHT-CAP WOVEN BY SPIDERS FROM THE NEW HEBRIDES.

This wonderful piece of work is spun entirely by spiders. The natives place a slight framework in some dark corner, which the spiders take possession of and use for their web, with the above marvellous result. The cap is 4ft. 10in. long and 1ft. 3in. wide at the base.

of loom weaving, and so there are not the same associations between spiders and woven cloth as exist in western cultures. Instead, there are echoes between the layers of spider webs and bark cloth, a type of layered cloth prevalent across Melanesia that is formed by sticking together layers of tree bark and beating them to form a type of stiff shell-like cloth. Spider web cloth is not stiff, it wraps and drapes around a body or object. It is durable, strong and waterproof — making it an ideal material for use in protecting, covering or carrying. In addition to creating 'hoods' the spider web fabric is used to create bags, to protect effigies, and as a mesh or support on which to construct conical masks. One of its most striking uses is as 'hair' on over-modelled skulls. These are highly sacred representations and embodiments of the dead, made by moulding a clay-like material onto the dead person's skull.

The spider web cloth is formed from webs spun by *Nephila plumipes* spiders and the smaller *Nephila pilipes*. Both are species of golden orb spider, and in the Botgate language of the area their webs are called *nangangao*. This term is used exclusively to describe the webs produced by these specific spiders, emphasising their importance in the formation and use of the spider cloth. As with the golden orb spider of Madagascar, their silk is a golden colour — yet this is dulled once the webs are layered together, along with dust and flies. In contrast to the aims of the spider silk weavers in Europe, in Malakula it is not the golden glow of the spider webs that is valued. Rather, it is the spiders themselves.

There is a particular form to the web of *Nephila* spiders that resonates with the appearance of depth in the layered spider web fabric. These spiders produce archetypal orb webs, strung up between branches, but the webs, and the spiders, are of such a large size that the spider must also create a series of support threads behind the spiral web. These webs are not on a single plane, as a European garden spider's web might appear to be, rather they extend backwards — they have depth, appearing as a mass of threads. When the spider web cloth is made, the sticky spiral

← Image of spider web 'nightcap' in *The Picture Magazine*, February 1896. It seems likely that this is a photograph of the same 'nightcap' as in the British Museum

threads of these webs bind together with the dry silk to form a fabric that still retains its depth, and the various bodies it has captured.

Collecting spider webs is the role of the men — women are not permitted to take part or even observe the process. Early in the morning, if they are the first that day to walk along a path through the jungle, the men take with them a frame made from a bamboo cane that has been split into strips to form a cone-like shape. Using a winding, twisting motion, they collect the spider webs they pass until a thick felt-like fabric has been formed. This is then knotted at the top and removed from the frame, at which point it can be beaten together with other webs to create a larger cloth. The men also collect the spiders and carry them in woven pandanus baskets back to the village, where they place them on barricades around the men's hut. There, the spiders will weave their giant webs, so that the hut is veiled from females and uninitiated males behind a glowing wall of silk.

Rather than being a 'smothering hood', the object in the Science Museum is a spider web headdress worn in male initiation ceremonies.

In this region there are two male grade systems: the *nimangki* society and the *nalawan* society. As a man rises up the ranks of the nimangki society, he will eventually be permitted to wear a spider web headdress. As he attains higher grades, the length of his spider web hood will increase. The headdresses are stored inside the walls of the men's hut, where the soot from the fire coats and blackens the spider silk.

The hood in the Science Museum is dull yellow, which suggests that it did not spend long enough in the men's hut to become blackened by soot, before it was taken by Mr Webb and sold at auction in London. It was brought from Vanuatu at the beginning of

← Split bamboo frame for collecting spider webs

the twentieth century when ethnographers were becoming increasingly interested in the cultures of Melanesia, which they felt were under threat from western influence. This was the period of 'salvage anthropology'.

In 1927, a year before the sale of the 'smothering hood', a Cambridge doctoral student, Arthur Bernard Deacon, wrote to his colleague in England, 'everything has gone, or is going, in the New Hebrides. I'm just getting what I can before it goes altogether'. Deacon had travelled to southwest Malakula as part of his ethnographic studies with the aim of recording what he believed to be the last days of these isolated cultures. Thanks to the influence of Anglo-French colonial rule, western religious and economic interests, and the deadly introduction of new viruses and diseases, the people and cultures of the South Pacific were in danger of disappearing forever. Ethnographers and anthropologists travelled to these islands not just to collect artefacts, but to record a whole people — languages, family relations, myths, and social systems. How and why do you record an entire people? The desire tells us as much about the ethnographer's culture as the one he's trying to observe.

After a year living in Malakula, and just a week before he was due to leave the island, Deacon died from fever. His copious notes, drawings and photographs were edited posthumously into a book entitled *Malekula: A Vanishing People in the New Hebrides*. His notebooks are held in the Royal Anthropological Institute in London. Full of sketches, notes and erasures, these contain Deacon's early attempts at recording sand-drawings, a Malakulan practice that has particular resonance with the creation and use of the spider web fabric. How Deacon and subsequent scholars recorded these drawings reveals the connections between how we draw and how we spin.

Sand-drawings are continuous flowing lines made in sand, dust or ashes and are usually created without the finger leaving the ground.

Often accompanied by storytelling and discussions, they are transient drawings — patterns in the sand that are then washed away by the tide or blown by the wind.

Various groups in Vanuatu may share what appears to be the same sand-drawing, but the stories that accompany them are different. Their value lies in the secret of how they are performed and explained, rather than the patterns themselves. The anthropologist Alfred Gell wrote that these intricate patterns are not to be considered as 'independent visual objects at all, but as performances, like dances, in which men could reveal their capability'. They exist on one spot, temporarily, emerging through action and movement, a pattern learned, repeated and handed down through generations.

How do you record a transient line? Deacon tried to copy them in pencil into his notebooks. His lines are hesitant, and the pages full of faded pencil marks that he's erased. Try copying one — keep your pen on the paper, or your finger in the sand, and keep the movement fluid making one continuous line. It's as if your eyes get in the way of the process, becoming caught in the pattern and making it stilted. Instead, focus on the movement of your hand, arm and body. Through repetition, it is the movement that is memorised, not the appearance of the pattern.

To help him see and record the patterns more clearly, Deacon asked for the drawings to be made in chalk on a blackboard, like a child in a classroom. He photographed these chalk drawings, and also those drawn in the sand. In the notebooks, his drawings become more confident with time, there is less rubbing out. Deacon wrote, 'These drawings are of course my own, and a good deal too accurate. They must not be taken for anything but 'ideal' figures. I hope to get photos of native drawings of these in white ashes on black earth'. He described them as 'too accurate' by which he means, *not accurate enough* — he has made them geometrically precise, fitting in to the grid of his notebook, but they are not able to fully record the patterns because they lack movement and they lack depth. If you draw a line in the sand it does not leave a flat single line like a pencil on paper. Instead, a sand-drawing is the thickness of your finger; it sinks into

A geometric design (sand drawing) on the ground at Seniang.
RAI 3859. Photograph by A.B. Deacon, early 1920s. © RAI

the grains and creates slight ridges either side as it moves. If you want to copy that line into your notebook, do you follow the line made by the left side of your finger, or the right side? Do you focus on the centre of the mark, the deepest line, or do you draw the shadow? The light changes, the wind blows, the tide turns and the drawing moves. It seems these same questions were going through Deacon's mind; in his early drawings he uses two parallel lines, as if to signify the indentation of the mark of a finger in the sand. These are later replaced by a single line.

After his death, Deacon's drawings and photographs of the sand-drawings were given to Mr C.O. Waterhouse at the British Museum to be copied for inclusion in a paper co-authored by Deacon's colleague Camilla Wedgwood. Entitled 'Geometrical Drawings from Malekula and Other Islands of the New Hebrides' it is a catalogue of sand-drawings that have been carefully copied from Deacon's drawings with ruler and compass. As it says in the footnotes, 'minor irregularities have been eliminated'. Each line within the patterns is numbered to show the order in which they are drawn, and some include a black dot to show the starting point. They resemble the dot-to-dot drawings in children's books, but with the lines already drawn in.[7]

The lines of the sand-drawings have gone through a series of transformations. If it were a sequence of events, it could have gone something like this:

1. A Malakulan man draws in the sand.
2. Deacon photographs the sand-drawing (in one of the photos a shadow of his sleeve appears).
3. The sand-drawing is eventually washed away by the tide or blown by the wind.
4. Deacon asks a Malakulan man to draw in chalk on a blackboard.
5. Deacon photographs the chalk drawing.
6. Deacon copies the sand-drawings in pencil in his notebooks.
7. Deacon makes more careful drawings from his initial sketches. Some of these include arrows to show the direction in which the lines are drawn, numbers to show the order they are drawn and the start and finishing points.
8. Mr Waterhouse creates geometric drawings from Deacon's sketches.
9. The drawings are recorded, catalogued and ready to be studied.

The sand-drawing has been preserved using typically western methods of fixing and recording: photographs and diagrams. But in Malakula, they were made to disappear. This is why sand-drawings are now protected by UNESCO as an example of 'intangible heritage'; it is not enough to catalogue the shape of the drawings, they exist only if the knowledge and power of their meaning is handed on and recreated.

---

7 These geometric representations of the sand-drawings by Waterhouse are reminiscent of diagrams showing how a spider builds its web, which can be seen in recent papers on animal behaviour. Because spiders leave a trail of silk wherever they go, tracking their movement along with the threads that will form the final web is a complex endeavour, and has to be simplified so that the angles, the sequence of building and comparisons between different webs can be measured.

A geometric design (sand drawing) on a blackboard
RAI 3864. Photograph by A.B. Deacon, early 1920s. © RAI

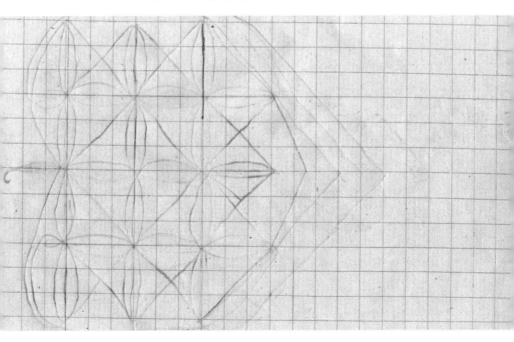

Erased sand drawing diagram in notebook.
MS 90/12/1 Photograph by A.B. Deacon, early 1920s. © RAI

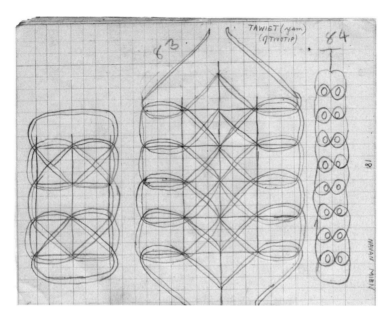

Sand drawing diagrams in notebook: (Nahal) Savsap; Tawiet
(yam); Navan Mien. MS 90/12/18 Photograph by A.B. Deacon,
early 1920s. © RAI

In addition to his sand-drawings there are other, livelier, lines in
Deacon's notebooks. In one, a worm has left its mark in the cover
— a short trail dug in to the cardboard, with some holes where the
worm has successfully broken through into pages beneath. Here
are Deacon's drawings of the landscape of Malakula. Some are
topographical, attempting to record the names of the bays, the
rocks, and the mountains. Others look as if they were made to pass
the time, to capture a view. The landscape drawings are tentative,
Deacon seemed unsure of how to describe the forms he is seeing, and
how to shade it with pencil marks — drawing vegetation is tiring,
nothing stands out to be drawn. He is bolder with the manmade
objects, the monuments, the carvings and buildings. Each has a firm
outline. And he is bold in his drawings of the Malakulans' ears — for
there are pages of them, divided from their owners and annotated

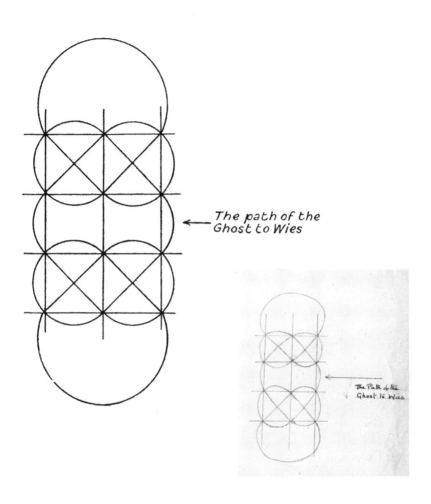

The path of the
Ghost to Wies

↑ Drawing by C.O. Waterhouse, in 'Geometrical Drawings
from Malekula and Other Islands of the New Hebrides'
A. Bernard Deacon and Camilla H. Wedgwood, *The Journal of
the Royal Anthropological Institute of Great Britain and Ireland*
64 (January 1, 1934)

→ Sand drawing diagram in notebook: The path of the Ghost
to Wies; 'Nahal' (Seniang); 'Lisevsep' (Big Nambas).
Photograph by A.B. Deacon, early 1920s. © RAI

with comments on the shapes of the folds and curves that each ear exhibits: people as puzzles to be studied and categorised. But the paper of these notebooks is thin and the drawings of previous pages can be seen, so that poking out between two ears (annotated with the comment 'very much overfolded helix') appears the faint outline of a statue with its semi-erect penis.

Sand-drawings depict figures, animals, and tales. In southwest Malakula, where the spider web fabric is made, sand-drawings are intimately linked to the figure of the spider, and the journey of the dead. When a person dies he travels down a forking path. One side is clear, while the other is blocked by a 'giant spider web' in which sits *Nendengele Hurae*: the spider spirit. Further on the journey, a guardian ghost, *Temes Savsap*, will test the dead person's knowledge of a half-finished sand-drawing. Only if the dead man can complete the sand-drawing can he proceed to the world of the dead, otherwise the spirit will devour him. In his examination of the sand-drawings, Deacon described the journey: 'As each ghost comes along the road the guardian ghost hurriedly rubs out one half of the figure. The ghost now comes up, but loses his track and cannot find it. He wanders about searching for a way to get past the Temes of the rock, but in vain. Only a knowledge of the completed geometrical figure can release him from this impasse. If he knows this figure, he at once completes the half which Temes Savsap rubbed out; and passes down the track through the middle of the figure. If, however, he does not know the figure, the Temes, seeing he will never find the road, eats him, and he never reaches the abode of the dead'. Although it is described as a 'labyrinth mythology', the dead man does not follow the line of the pattern looking for an exit, rather the route which the dead must take lies 'between the two halves' of the drawing — a route which Deacon notes on his drawings with an arrow. The secret of escaping the guardian ghost lies in *mirroring*, in completing the half-obscured sand-drawing. The labyrinth cannot be followed like a maze or a thread

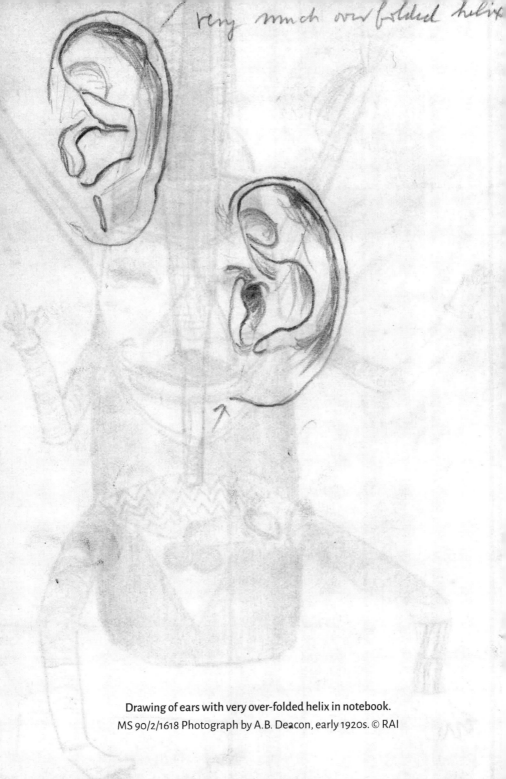

very much over-folded helix

Drawing of ears with very over-folded helix in notebook.
MS 90/2/1618 Photograph by A.B. Deacon, early 1920s. © RAI

but can only be escaped through reflection. The pattern the dead man draws is a shadow of the other half.

Once the man has entered the world of the dead he can then revisit the world of the living. For within this region of Malakula, the dead and the living are never entirely distinct, but rather exist at once together. The higher a man rises up the ranks of society, and so is permitted to wear the spider web headdress, the closer he becomes to the honourable status of 'living-dead' man. Death is not conceived as the cutting of the thread of life, as in the Classical myth of the Fates. Rather, it seems to echo the 'all at once' of the indivisible layers of the spider web cloth. Death exists with 'the powers of generation' wrote the anthropologists Remo Guidieri and Francesco Pellizzi in their study of the 'cult of the dead' in Malakula. Just as the spider's web is produced only because the spider has eaten, and the spider only eats because the web has trapped its prey, the cyclical motion of life and death, and life *in* death, occurs in the process of making the spider web cloth. Each evening the spider eats its web and builds a new one, which by morning might be gathered with others on a bamboo frame and taken back to the village.

Alfred Gell described the effects of patterns such as sand-drawings as 'mind-traps' in which we become caught. He gave the example of a Celtic knot pattern, used to repel demons by trapping them within its continuous and intricate line. The demon is visually and mentally attracted to the pattern, intrigued by how it is formed, and through this curiosity he is forever caught within the knot. For Gell, patterns were not simply decorative additions to the surface of an object. Or, more correctly, patterns *are* decorative, but Gell argued that decorations are not unnecessary flourishes — rather, they act upon how we perceive the object and the person who made it. Decorative patterns are a method of attachment between bodies and things. We look at a pattern and become entranced. We are stopped in our tracks — frowning, peering, trying to make sense of what we see and how it was made. The object and its maker have captured us. Gell termed this effect of patterns as 'cognitive stickiness'.[8]

There's a seductive link here with the spider. Its web is a pattern that entraps. But go closer into the web, to the sticky capture thread: formed of equally spaced bundles of silk held inside a viscous solution, this is a material that entangles and sticks at once. Only some spiders have the capacity to create sticky silk, and it seems likely that this material evolved from the neurotransmitters of their ancestors. Sticky spider silk was once, literally, cognitive stickiness. Chemicals and processes that formed the internal workings of a spider's nervous system became a material with which later species would build their external world.

Sticky cognition links to the physical patterns of our own thoughts: the connections between neurotransmitters in the brain. These are plastic processes; new links can be grown through learning, while others are cut off through lack of use. We preserve our energy for useful pattern making, forming and reforming in constant relation to our environment. To be stuck in a pattern is to be mentally stuck, to be limited by our own knowledge, skills and experience. The frequent mislabelling of Malakulan headdresses within British museums may in part be due to a historical lack of attention to how these artefacts are made and used, but the confusion over how the spider web fabric was made suggests an imaginative block. The collectors of these artefacts in the early twentieth century must have known that spider webs can be sticky, and a brief examination of the spider headdress reveals that it is formed of layers

---

8 In 'Technology and Magic', Gell discusses a particular example of sticky spider silk and entrapment in its use as fishing lures in parts of Papua New Guinea (see colour insert: Fig 12). He writes of this practice, 'Fish in the lagoon would see the sparkling spider's web ball and mistake it for an insect. But when they bit into it the sticky spider's web would cause their jaws to adhere to one another, so that they could not let go.' The fish were probably needlefish, or garfish, which have a long jaw and pointed teeth. Rather than adhering to the sticky spider's silk, it is more likely that the fish were visually attracted to the spider silk lure, which may also have been dipped in bait. The fish were then caught either by net or hook. In this region, fishing kites are sometimes used rather than rods. Fishermen fly these from boats, with a lure attached by a thread to the end of the kite. The movement of the kite in the wind creates the impression underwater of a glittering shoal of fish.

of webs. Yet this way of making fabrics is not immediately apparent to the collectors: some think that the headdress is formed entirely by spiders, others believe it is made entirely by humans. Here's the sticking point: faced with a pattern of entangled threads, if you come from a culture that associates spiders with weaving and shimmering fabric, can you see a different technique — can you see a different way of seeing?

The hood invites you to touch it. Its patterning is not just a visual entrapment, it is a tactile one; what would such a thing feel like on your hair, your skin?

Between 2009 and 2010, the British artist Kira O'Reilly created a series entitled *Webskins* in which she photographed sticky spider webs placed on parts of her body (see colour insert: Fig 9 and 10). In the images the tiny hairs that cover her skin are visible, touching and piercing the web. 'I do like the suggestion of stocking tops, the hairs on my skin which mimic the hairs on the spiders and all of that stuff about hairy femininities, you know how glossy and super airbrushed mainstream super femme body is, so I like the up too close and personal of the saggy skin of my body and the saggy skin of the webs on it'. The webs she uses are sticky and full of the bodies they have caught. The hairs on her skin respond to the touch of the web, reaching out so that they appear at once like the hairs of a spider, but also like hundreds of spider legs. There is something wonderfully hesitant about these photographs. The touch of the spider web is not directly on the skin; rather, it floats above it on a bristling layer of hairs, each delaying the possibility of skin/web contact.

O'Reilly discusses this series in relation to the word 'felt', to describe both a material made by layering, and the sensation of touch. The fabric of felt is traditionally formed of damp woollen fibres that have been entangled together through a process of rubbing and rolling. Like the layered spider web fabric, felt is not a woven material, nor does it create an unbroken material plane. It invites more threads to join in the entanglement. O'Reilly writes that the *Webskins* images remind her of 'those covert spaces in between body and clothing'. In the moment of being worn, human hairs and spider webs entangle, creating this other secret layer between skin and silk.

In O'Reilly's images, the web has the appearance of a second skin or healing gauze. They suggest a protective yet breathable skin that is not entirely distinct from the body it covers, echoing perhaps one of the oldest uses of spider web as a dressing for wounds and ailments. It is possible that the antibacterial properties of spider web helped in the healing process, and staunched the flow of blood.[9] In his *Naturalis Historia* Pliny the Elder also recommends the use of a cobweb as a compress on the forehead, which, he writes, 'is marvellously useful for the cure of defluxions of the eyes'. It is difficult to trace the history and decline of this medicinal use of spider webs. These wound dressings are free, readily available, and easily discarded, and the silken threads of a spider web dressing become indivisible from human hair, skin and blood.

This melding of body and web resonates with an obscure historical technique known as 'cobweb painting'. Developed in the Tyrolean Alps during the mid-seventeenth century, spider webs were used as canvases for small watercolour paintings. Around a hundred of these 'cobweb paintings' have survived. Early versions tended to depict religious themes. An example hangs in Chester Cathedral. It shows the Madonna and Child, painted on a skin of silk.[10]

---

9 The healing potential of spider web extended into the early nineteenth century, when a Dr Broughton of Wisconsin University prescribed spider web as 'pills' to feverish patients. Spiders themselves were also ingested as cures, or hung alive around the neck inside a walnut to cure fever. It is unclear why spiders and their webs were used as cures for fever: perhaps the shaking of a spider on its web mimicked the shaking of a feverish patient.

10 There is some disagreement over whether the Chester cobweb painting is on spider silk or caterpillar silk. The Cathedral describes it as caterpillar silk, while the arachnologist W.G. Bristowe in *The World of Spiders* cites it as an example of painting on spider silk.

'Love and devotion were their incentives', wrote the art historian Ina Cassirer of the Tyrolean cobweb painters, 'the more fragile [the paintings] were, the more they were cherished'. In addition to the value placed on the fragility of the canvas, they were usually framed so that they could be viewed from both sides. Often placed in windows, this had the effect of making the religious image float in a halo of webs as it caught the light. Like the stained glass windows of a church, the figures in a cobweb painting seem to glow with life.

The effect of spider webs in a frame mirrors that of the barriers of spider webs used in south Malakula to both obscure the view of the men's huts, and emphasise the power within. But unlike these screens, the cobweb paintings display an uneasy relationship with their material. As Cassirer describes, while the early paintings were made of spider webs, these were soon replaced by the web of the caterpillar *Hyponomeuta evonymella* whose canvases were not as 'dirty' as those of a spider. In spite of this material change, the cobweb painters often included a small image of a spider in the corner of their paintings 'to call attention to the material and to the exceptional skill required to paint on it'. As with the embroidered spiders on the golden cape in the last chapter, there is an odd back and forth between avoiding the sticky and 'dirty' aspects of spiders, while also asserting the desirable qualities of spider silk. The value of the cobweb paintings relies on an embrace and denial of the material.

Although cobweb painting died out in the early nineteenth century, there was a revival of the technique a century later. Rather than depicting religious icons, these tended to be paintings of women and flowers and were sold as souvenirs to tourists. The cobweb painting entitled 'S'Nandi' (see colour insert: Fig 6, 7 and 8) was made by an anonymous artist in the early twentieth century. The full picture shows a smiling young woman, her face framed with wisps of gentle curls. Beside this are two magnified photographs of the painting, the top one showing her left eye and the lower a detail of one of the pearls around her neck. This shrinking of scale reveals the entangled mesh of lines that hold her appearance,

→ Man clothed from head to feet in a tunic of spider's web.
RAI 3850 Photograph by A.B. Deacon, early 1920s. © RAI

RAI 3851 Photograph by A.B. Deacon, early 1920s. ©RAI

crisscrossing her face, her clothes, her hair, and her eyeballs. It is as if the webs in Kira O'Reilly's work are finally indivisible from the woman's skin.

The spider web headdress in the Science Museum has never lost its ability to capture. Through sticky accumulation it can grow, perhaps capturing a strand of hair fallen from the head of a Museum visitor. Originally made to be worn and move, what do these objects do all day? They are wrapped in acid-free paper, inside a box in a storage room. Occasionally, for conservation reasons, they have to be cleaned. This cannot be done with water, as they would shrink. Instead, the conservator removes any dust with a vacuum cleaner and might then individually tweeze out any detritus stuck in the web. The culture of preserving objects is such that in certain contexts it is someone's job to remove flies from a spider's web.

Among Deacon's notebooks are two photographs, possibly taken during a funerary ritual in Malakula. They are of a man dressed in a tunic made entirely from spider webs. It covers his head and face and falls to just above his feet. There are two holes for his eyes, and attached to the body of the tunic are two horned masks. On his arms he wears two long stiff looking tubes that end in what appear to be white gloves. The photographs are taken seconds apart, his arms appearing more outstretched in one, as if taking flight.[11] We can see that he is standing still because the trees behind him are blurred in the wind. The photograph is reminiscent of the model wearing the woven golden spider silk cape. But unlike the static pose of the female model, the man in the spider web tunic is only held for a moment by the camera before he moves to continue his dance in the funerary ritual, 'a veritable play of mirrors where dead presences and their more or less ephemeral effigies appear and disappear'. For Gell, the movement of a Malakulan dance is itself a type of drawing, a negotiation of a maze in which the man weaves his own invisible fabric with a continuous line of movement. And if the dance can be seen as a drawing of threads, so the drawings are themselves a type of dance — perhaps, Gell writes, even a type of music; a harmony of voices, in which we can hear many layers, but cannot disentangle one from all the others.

---

11 The pose of the figure in these photographs echoes the funerary mannequins that are specific to this area. Known as rambaramps, these are created as doubles of the dead man. The head is moulded from a vegetative compost onto the dead man's skull, the body is formed of tree fern and bamboo, and the rambaramp's hair is formed of spider web fabric. With his similar appearance to a rambaramp, the figure in the photograph resembles a resemblance of death — it mimics the pose of a figure that acts as the double of a dead man.

Fig 1

Fig 2

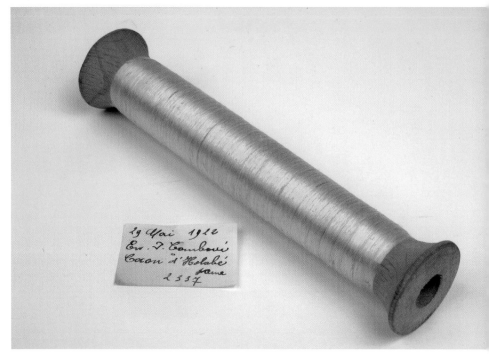

Fig 3

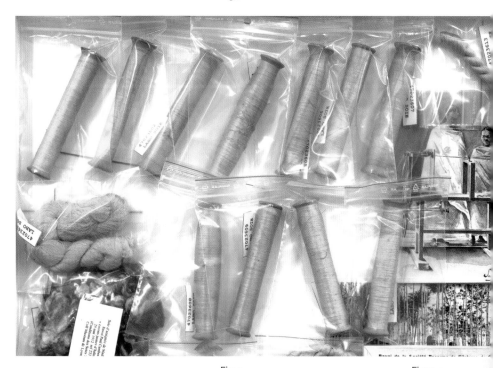

Fig 4   Fig 5 →

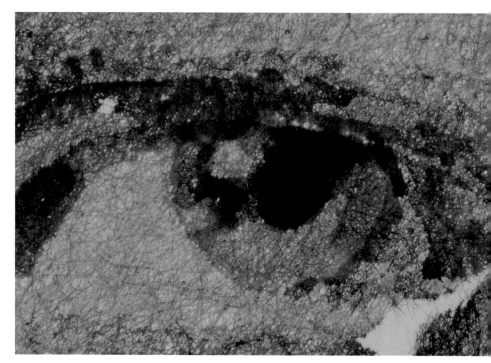

Fig 6

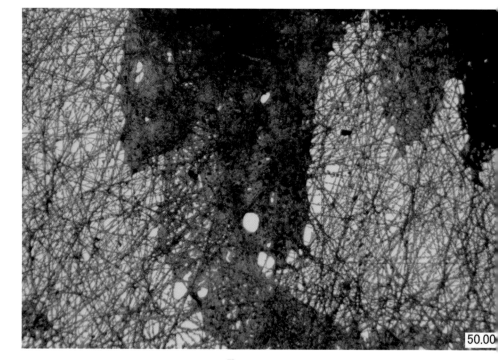

50.00

Fig 7

Fig 8

Fig 9

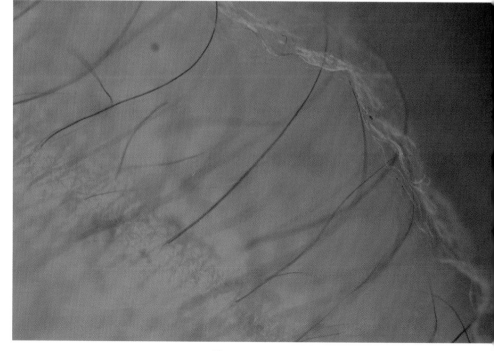

Fig 10   Fig 11 →

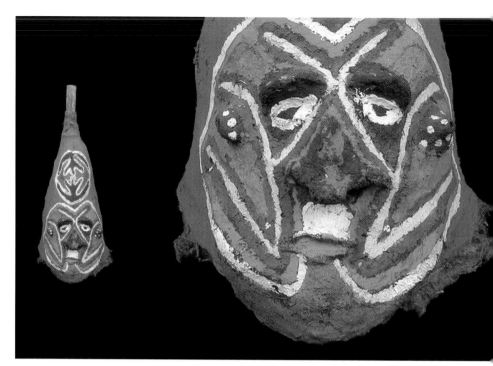

Fig 12

Fig 13

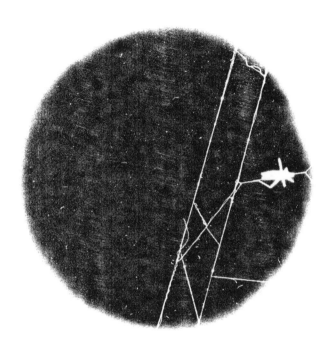

Vibrating

My eyes are blind, my ears filled with humming, and
sweat streams down my body, I am seized by a sudden
shuddering; I turn greener than grass, and in a moment
more, I feel I shall die
Sappho, Fragment 31

I am in the research rooms of the Pitt Rivers Museum in Oxford looking at a very thin collection entitled *Five Spider Egg Cases in a Paper Envelope*. It is impossible to grasp. I poke my gloved hand inside the walls of the 1930s envelope trying to remove the white, flat spider egg cases inside. But they are more attracted to the sides and corners of the envelope than my dull fingers. I gently blow on them and the five silken skins float onto the table.

The spider egg cases were spun by a female wall crab spider, *Selenopidae*. This family consists of a few hundred species that exist in subtropical and tropical regions. They are extremely fast moving, pouncing on their prey with great speed. To add to the surprise, they are also particularly well camouflaged with brownish grey colouring. As such, they have been described as 'among the most secretive of animals'. One aspect of their lives, however, is very visible and that is the egg cases that the females weave. These appear as thin white discs,

Selenopidae egg case

up to five centimetres in diameter, which the female attaches to trees or buildings. They are formed of fibres of silk that the spider layers together with gluey secretions to create a strong surface with which to protect her eggs. Although it is composed of numerous threads, the egg case appears to the human eye as a smooth plane. It resembles a thin layer of skin, an animal membrane.

Henry Balfour, the first curator of the Pitt Rivers Museum, collected the five spider egg cases in 1938 from an area around Victoria Falls. Balfour was particularly interested in the history and development of a group of musical instruments known as mirlitons. These are acoustic instruments that are composed of tubes with an attached membrane, such as a kazoo. When the user sings or speaks down the tube, the stretched membranes vibrate and create a buzzing sound in sympathy with the human voice. In parts of Europe, membranes of mirlitons were historically made from onion skins or animal intestines. However, in regions of West and Central Africa the most common material used for vibrating membranes are the egg cases of spiders. These skins of silken threads buzz, screech and hum with the human voice, for they are formed of a material that is primed for receiving and transmitting vibrations.

A few spiders, such as ogre-faced or jumping spiders, use vision to find their prey. Most spiders, however, have relatively poor eyesight and must use their acoustic-vibratory senses to detect and communicate with the world around them. A spider's body is covered in tiny hairs. Some of these are relatively springy and are known as tactile hairs, each attached to a nerve, which allow the spider a sense of touch. Others are stiff and are known as trichobothria or filiform hairs. These are used to sense vibrations in the air and are of different lengths, each attuned to a different frequency. They act like individual microphones with a frequency range from 40 to 600 Hertz, depending on the length of hair. A unit of hertz describes how often something vibrates in a second. To a human ear, 40Hz sounds like the low hum produced by electrical speakers, while 600Hz sounds like the buzz of a mosquito. In general, humans can hear up to around 20,000Hz, so have a far greater range than spiders. But spiders have evolved to pick up only the vibrations that are relevant to their survival — that of approaching prey, predator or mate.

In addition to these hairy microphones that sense vibrations in the air, spiders have tiny parallel slits in their exoskeleton known as lyriform organs. If the material on which the spider is sitting vibrates, whether it's a thread of silk or the living-room carpet, these vibrations will carry through spider's claws and up its leg joints where the lyriform slits will contract and stretch in response. The spider can then sense whether a fly has landed on its web — in which case, a quick response is needed — or if it's just a fallen leaf.

A female garden spider can usually be found in one of two places. She will either sit at the centre of her web, with each leg positioned on a radial thread, or she will extend a line of silk from the centre up into a leaf or shelter where she will sit with one leg extended on this signal line,

ready to quickly drop into the web if she senses the vibrations of her prey. Sometimes the flies hanging in the web are not moving. To locate these, and to differentiate desirable prey from a fallen leaf, the spider will pluck at the radial strands of the web with her front legs. This action might appear to resemble the tugging of a fishing line, but rather than testing the tension of the strand, the spider is sensing possible changes in the vibratory echo of its web. She is plucking a thread and then 'listening' to changes in the returning vibrations.

Vibrating silk is vital to the courtship serenade of garden spiders, with the males plucking out their specific rhythm on the female's web. But acoustic sense and touch is used by all species to communicate, and many male spiders will court the female using vibrations. The house spider *Tegenaria*, the large brown spiders that tend to be found in bathtubs or running from under the television, are funnel-web spiders. Instead of creating an orb web, they spin a mass of delicate sticky threads that form a tube in which the spider sits. The male will approach a female slowly, and as he does so he will tap out a rhythm on her web using the palps on the front of his head, like a drumroll. This tapping will continue up to the moment that he mates, when he will begin stroking the female with his legs. Stroking is a common activity in many spider species during courtship and mating.

Spider silk is therefore not just a material with which to capture or protect, it a vibrating line of communication. And this is why it has been such a useful material for making acoustic instruments. If Henry Balfour hadn't collected them from Africa and brought them back to Oxford, then the five spider egg cases in the Pitt Rivers museum could have been used to make one of two types of instruments: a hunting lure or a voice disguiser; instruments used to communicate with animals and supernatural beings.

In the British Museum is an example of a spider silk hunting lure, made by the Bemba people of Central Africa and donated to the Museum in the 1970s. It is defined in the Museum catalogue as a duiker lure, but Balfour writes that the Bemba name for the instrument is 'chinyenye'. Duikers are small antelopes common to sub-Saharan Africa. The lure is made from the horn of a male duiker that has been cut to create a tube of about 4 centimetres in length. One end is open, while the other end is covered by the membrane of a spider's egg case. There is no record of how the membrane is attached to the horn, but in similar objects rubber, gum or wax is used to keep the membrane taut.

To play the lure, the open end is held horizontally against the lower lip and then blown across. I am only allowed to examine the lure while wearing gloves, so it is not possible to describe how the object feels, and it is certainly not possible for me to actually play the instrument. A description of what it sounds like, therefore, must be taken from other witnesses. Reverend R.D. Macminn, a missionary based in the area during the early twentieth century, describes the sound produced by the chinyenye as a 'short, shrill scream'. Only the initiated males of the

Bemba are allowed to use this lure. When it is blown, the membrane of spider silk vibrates like a drum skin, emitting the 'scream'. This sounds like a young duiker in distress, so that other duikers run to its aid and the hunters can capture them. The lure resembles its prey: it is both formed of the antelope and mimics its sound.

To play the lure at its loudest, so that the antelopes can hear it far away, it is necessary to hit the 'right' note. The force of the hunter's breath across the hole of the tube must match the spider silk's resonant frequency — that is the speed at which it naturally vibrates. The spider silk sounds in sympathetic vibration to the hunter's voice.

In other parts of West and Central Africa spider web egg cases are used to create instruments for a different purpose: to conjure the voices of spirits and dead ancestors. Known as 'voice disguisers', they are tubes with a hole in the middle and a spider silk at the end. Rather than blowing across the hole, as with the duiker lure, the user speaks or sings into it. This produces what Balfour describes as a '"reedy" or "nasal" intonation'.

The Igbo of South Nigeria make voice disguisers from reed tubes, which are used by masked performers to simulate 'the voices of ancestral or other spirits'. Even when they are being played, these instruments are hidden by the performers from women and uninitiated men. Edward Lifschitz, curator and anthropologist at the Smithsonian Museum, described the masked performers as 'emissaries from some aspect of the spirit world'

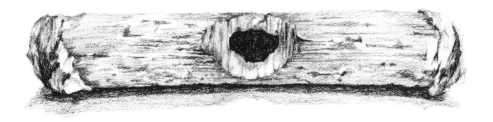

A voice disguiser made in southern Nigeria with a spider egg case membrane attached at either end of a tube.

Image by Henry Balfour with the description 'Masked performers in Maw ceremonies, Ibo tribe, S. Nigeria' in B.M. Blackwood and Henry Balfour, 'Ritual and Secular Uses of Vibrating Membranes as Voice-Disguisers', *The Journal of the Royal Anthropological Institute of Great Britain and Ireland* 78, no. 1/2 (January 1, 1948).

that can only speak through the medium of the vibrating spider web. The instrument disguises the performer's voice, altering it with a buzzing layer of sound, but the masked figures will also speak in unfamiliar and foreign languages making it more difficult for the uninitiated to understand. In these cases, a designated speaker accompanying the masquerade will translate the words of the masked figures to the assembled audience. In this case, the voice disguiser is hidden while the masked performers are visible as the source of the sound. But the men of the Dan people of Liberia and the Mbuti of the Democratic Republic of Congo use voice disguisers to create sounds of the supernatural without any visible human presence. They are used at night, when women and uninitiated men must remain inside their houses ignorant of the source of the sounds. The buzzing calls of the spirit world float and fly in all directions, boundless across the village.

The use of spider egg cases as vibrating membranes may be an example of people using what is to hand. But there's a further association between spiders and buzzing in the stories of the West African spider trickster Ananse, that suggest that something about making nasally, buzzing sounds allows silent or inaudible beings to be heard.

Anansesem, or spider stories, is the name given to the tales told by the Akan people of Ghana. Even if the spider trickster Ananse does not feature, the act of telling tales is a spidery activity. He is the bringer of stories and wisdom and, as with other trickster figures, he may succeed in his plans through playful subversion, or fail through his own selfishness and arrogance. Trying to tie down Ananse and define him, or even to list all his tales, is itself a foolish endeavour. He is wonderfully contradictory and keeps shifting. In some tales Ananse lives in human society, has a wife and children, exhibits human behaviours of weakness, selfishness, pride, and envy. And yet... he may also jump onto the ceiling, walk on water and have the bald head of a spider creature. He is human and spider and neither one nor the other, able to move between human, animal and supernatural forms and worlds. Akan royal spokesmen carry staffs on which is carved a spider in its web. It is a symbol of language, not in the fixed sense of officialdom, but in the play of spoken word, the double-entendre, language as game, wit as trap.

When Ananse speaks he speaks with a buzz, a nasal tone. Rather than using a membrane of spider silk to create the buzz, the person speaking as Ananse will use the membranes of the human throat to block and transform his normal speaking voice. As a figure that mediates between worlds, the nasal sounds of the spider trickster seem to echo the use of buzzing in the voice-disguisers. The anthropologist Philip Peek suggests that it is the apparent silence of spiders that seems to make them suitable for their role as a trickster. He asks whether such animals are 'more likely to speak like and with spiritual beings if they are not normally "heard" in this world'?

The sympathetic vibrations of membranes, whether spider silk or human skin, can distort the normal sound of the voice, but in doing so create a layer of more powerful, supernatural meaning. In this sense, the

Image by Henry Balfour of a performer playing the nyastaranga. in B.M. Blackwood and Henry Balfour, 'Ritual and Secular Uses of Vibrating Membranes as Voice-Disguisers', *The Journal of the Royal Anthropological Institute of Great Britain and Ireland* 78, no. 1/2 (January 1, 1948).

spider silk membrane acts as both a mirror to the voice, and its screen — both enhancing and blocking the sound of the human. Materials and bodies vibrate in response to each other as an accumulation of audible and inaudible sounds. Just as there is no buzzing without the human voice, so the sound of the spirit world cannot be heard without the vibration of the silk.

Human throat and spider silk come together in another musical instrument, one so mysterious that there's some doubt among scholars whether it even existed. It originated in northern India and is called a 'nyastaranga'. It was made of two individual long metal horns, similar to a hunting horn. Stretched across the mouthpiece of each was a spider silk egg case. What makes this instrument unique is that the player would hold the mouthpieces of the horns against his neck, and hum so that the vibrations of his throat were transformed through the vibrating spider silk and out of the end of the horns. The ethnomusicologist Charles Capwell describes a nineteenth century musician, Kaliprasanno Bandyopadhyay, who 'achieved international fame' for his playing of the nyastaranga. It was apparently a very difficult instrument to play, and he suffered from breathing problems throughout his life.

Duiker lures and voice disguisers make explicit use of the vibratory potential of spider silk to create sounds and to attract prey. But in Western Europe, it is human music that attracts spiders. In France and England during the early nineteenth century a group of tales surfaces of spiders attracted to human music and song. These have no clear point of origin, but are repeated down the years, appearing in books on music, and miscellaneous facts about spiders. One story is that of a French Captain in the 18th century, who had been imprisoned for insubordination. To pass the hours in jail, he would play his lute each evening. After a few minutes of playing he was astonished to see spiders descend from their webs in the cell and form a circle around him, only to return to their homes when he finished playing. The prisoner 'began to give a concert to these animals, who seemed to come every day in greater numbers, as though they had invited others, so that in the course of time he found a hundred gather about him'.

In *A General History of the Science and Practice of Music*, John Hawkins describes a man in the 18th century who would play the violin every evening by candlelight. Hawkins writes that as this man played, he saw 'several spiders descend from the ceiling, who came and ranged themselves about the table to hear him play ... they remained upon the table very attentively until somebody came to tell him supper was ready. When having ceased to play, he told me these insects remounted their webs, to which he would suffer no injury to be done. It was a diversion with which he often entertained himself out of curiosity'.

These two stories feature occasionally in books, but the tale repeated most often in contemporary reports concerns a group of schoolgirls in the early nineteenth century in Kensington, West London. Each day, during hymn practice at their boarding school, huge spiders would descend from the ceiling and hang about these girls as they sang. Once the girls had finished singing, the spiders would retreat back to their webs in the rafters.

The earliest version of this story appears in the popular magazine *The Mirror of Literature, Amusement, and Instruction* in January 1836:

'Many anecdotes have been related to prove that spiders are fond of music, and here is another: At a well-known ladies' school at Kensington, an immense kind of spider is common... The young ladies by no means admire these visiters [sic], who, when according to the custom of the house, they are all singing a verse or two of a hymn or psalm, before morning and evening prayers, then generally make their appearance on the floor, or suspended overhead from their thick webs in the ceiling, obviously, and a fact not to be contradicted, attracted from their hiding places in the old room by the harmonious "concord of sweet sounds".

The story is published almost unchanged in articles over the following years. There is no date given for these events, other than the date of the magazine article, and there is no information to locate the school or the girls.

When I first came across this tale, I wanted objects to support it — documents, diaries, pictures — something that would give solidity to the story, and an identity to these singing girls, whose days appeared to have been bookended by hymns, prayers and spiders. In spite of their power to enchant spiders from the ceiling with their voices, they seemed a silent group — moving obediently from morning to evening.

I looked into girls' schools that existed in this period, and narrowed it down to Aubrey House in Kensington, a ladies' boarding school that is now a set of luxury apartments. Only a few records remain of this school and its singing girls.

At the Kensington library is a set of pencil drawings made in the mid nineteenth century by a pupil at Aubrey house called Euphemia Johnston. She drew them in the final years of the school before it closed in 1854. Although they were created after the spider article first appeared, these

Little Jessie Hay in bed in the corner room. Drawing by
Euphemia Johnston, March 1852

were the only objects I was able to find that gave some insight into the
lives of these singing, silent girls. At first, I attempted to trace Euphemia
Johnston herself. I followed her in online records (or someone who
shared her name) to her birth in Suffolk, her marriage straight after
leaving school and her death in Scotland. I felt I was moving in the
wrong direction, or perhaps not listening or looking in the right way. It
seemed it was the drawings themselves on which I should focus — not
as objects that might solidify a tale into fact, but as things that might
resonate with spiders, singing and silken lines.

Euphemia's first drawing, made in March 1852, is of 'Little Jessie Hay
in bed in the corner room'. Little Jessie Hay is shrunk by her surroundings,
by so much drapery. Is she ill, perhaps, or has the older girl told her to
keep still while she practises her drawing skills? Half of Jessie's face
pokes out of the covers, drawn flat and tiny, looking directly at Euphemia.
But it is the drawing itself that strikes me: it is a teenage drawing.
By this I mean that she is following certain taught rules of drawing,

Vibrating

The Perspective Class. Drawing by Euphemia Johnston,
September, 1852

such as perspective, shading, and changing the pressure of the line to
create depth, but she is carrying these out with such careful concern and
attention that certain objects go awry — a chair, the bed stand, the jug.
Everything is outlined; there are no gaps for the viewer to fill in. The lines
where the walls meet the ceiling appear drawn with a ruler, but then
overlaid with a freehand line to give it liveliness. Euphemia is probably
right-handed, as the direction of the shading lines in the drawing are the
most comfortable angle at which to move a right hand across a page. In
some areas, the shading represents shadow and depth, but on the back
wall they describe simply a need to fill in the blank space. Nothing but
loose shading is seen through the window, it is an entirely interior scene.

Her next drawing entitled 'The Perspective Class', gives a clue to
where Euphemia has been learning her lines. At first, I notice the
woman facing, with her awkward face and hands. Her hair and that
of her companions seems to have been more pleasurable to draw: flows
of small lines going from light to dark and curling around the face and

Miss Shepheard and Miss Caroline in mysterious conference.
Drawing by Euphemia Johnston, October 23, 1853

neck. Again the lines of furniture and the walls and windows have been drawn with a ruler, but freer lines appear — the gathered clothes of the women, the bend of the table legs, the painting of the dog and the leaves through the window. And in the corner of the room, overlaid on a ruled line, is a loose line hanging down from the ceiling and ending in a ball: a bell pull perhaps, or an echo of the hanging spiders.

A year later, she draws two women 'in mysterious conference'. Less important objects are fading into the background. Instead, Euphemia is

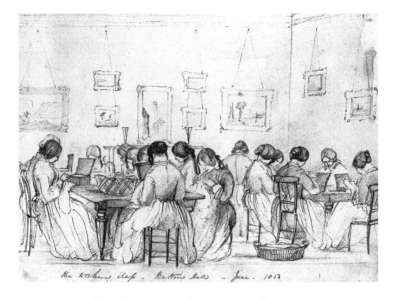

The Working Class. Drawing by Euphemia Johnston, June 1854

focused on the two women: the curl of their hair and the tilt of the heads. The way the woman facing slightly bends her neck towards the other, a familiar female position, used to listen, whisper, and console. The other girl is speaking perhaps, the one whose face is obscured by the curl of hair. She is the one who is suffering or sharing a secret. The dresses are described with quick, enjoyable whips of lines, following a curve. And again, just behind their heads, hangs the 'spider'.

Euphemia's final drawing is all hair and necks and draping cloth. She describes it as 'The Working Class' and it appears to me as a silent room, except for the sound of cloths moving, and the inaudible movement of embroidery threads. All the girls have their heads down, focusing on their work, while above them hang fading paintings of landscapes. The room is barely sketched in; the focus is on the girls and everything they touch.

These four drawings could be categorised as examples of 'feminine accomplishments' in England during the nineteenth century. Drawing, embroidery, singing and piano playing were taught to upper- and middle-class girls as appropriate skills for obedient daughters and future wives.

None of these skills, however, was meant to lead to any professional application — they were private rather than public achievements. Made by a young woman, Euphemia's drawing are certainly not typically considered part of art history — historical records perhaps, showing the lives of girls at nineteenth century boarding schools. But taken seriously as drawings, as the artist certainly did, they reveal a development in skills and confidence. Her approach to drawing is particularly that of a teenager or young woman — a certain care, earnestness, privacy and romance.

The singing girls and their spiders were beginning to make sounds, but I wanted to hear them better. I decided to conduct my own spider serenade.

As a teenager, I liked to play the piano in a romantic way. I sat with excellent posture, a slight incline of the neck and a light touch. I would also sing to the quiet, but admiring, gathering of imaginary people. My song of choice was Robert Burns' poem, 'My love is like a red, red rose', which I would repeat again and again because it was never quite good enough. I had inherited an attitude to feminine accomplishments that would not have been out of place over a century before. With Euphemia's drawings in mind, Robert Burns' poem seemed to be the perfect song for me to sing to a spider.

I wanted the serenade to take place indoors, in the drawing-room, so I first had to collect a spider and its web. I created a large wooden frame on a stand, which leant slightly back. This was a similar angle to the one at which a spider builds its web — it is never entirely vertical. I wanted it to be an attractive place for spiders. I found a female *Araneus diadematus* in the garden and placed it on the edge of this frame. I then left it outside overnight. The angle was apparently perfect, as by morning it had spun a web inside the frame and was hanging in the centre. I brought the whole thing inside, and placed it in front of me on a table: face-to-face with the spider.

When attempting to communicate with a spider you need to assess what part of your body vibrates the most. Put your hand to your lips and speak. The lips move, but the vibrations are coming from somewhere deeper. Speak again, and put your hand to the front of

Serenading a spider

your throat. Here, under the skin, is your larynx. Two thin layers of skin that vibrate as the air from your lungs is pushed through them, and which tighten and loosen to change the pitch of your tune, without you having to think of their tightening. It is here where the skin seems to vibrate the most. Although the girls in Kensington could entice spiders through the air with their singing, I wanted a more solid line of communication with the spider. I had collected some dragline silk from spider webs around the garden and twisted and wove these together to create a long spider silk choker which I tied around my throat. At its centre I attached a long thread of spider silk and hooked the other end onto a radial spoke of the spider's web in the frame. Sitting in front of the framed web, it resembled a tapestry at which I worked. I was now connected by my neck to the spider's web.

I tried to sit still, but I couldn't stop the involuntary movements of my body — slight twitches, the pulse in my neck, my breathing — and these the spider could sense even when I was silent. She could also sense the change in air currents that I created when I breathed out, using the tiny hairs on her body. I began to hum, practising my scales, and then I sang my serenade.

Sometimes she did nothing; she simply sat motionless in the middle of her web. Sometimes she tensed up her legs, plucking at the web to find the origin of the vibrations. But most terrifyingly for me she would sometimes shoot towards the thread of silk by which I was connected and grab it, slowly walking towards my neck. The sight and feel of a spider sitting three inches from my throat, a part of my body invisible to me, was too much. My heart raced, my breathing turned to panting, and I began to sweat. With shaking hands, I broke the silk bridge that connected us, and she raced back to the centre of her web.

What is this fear? It felt almost like a shrinking. When faced with a spider heading towards my throat, it was not that the spider suddenly became huge, rather that I felt I was reduced entirely to the size of my voice box — the vibrating point, invisible to me, to which she was heading.

People with severe spider phobia often describe these alterations of scale. They tend to perceive spiders as unnaturally large, or themselves shrunk to the size of the spider's prey. A repeated fear is that the spider will invade the inside of their body. In a series of interviews with spider phobics, one woman reports that the worst thing is, 'probably the... the feeling that, you think about the feeling if it actually got onto you, onto your skin, the feeling of the legs on the skin'. It is not the spider's bite that is horrific, but its light and scurrying touch. Like the gentle stroke of Nosferatu's nails along your cheek, it is a moment of anticipation: something horrific will follow. But it is also dreadful because it is the same touch as that of the seducer; a touch that barely touches, causing a rush of blood and shakes of expectation.

In my spider serenade, why did she sometimes respond, and sometimes do nothing? It could be that I occasionally hit certain frequencies that resonated with her — that were transformed through the silk bridge and her legs into the frequency of a buzzing fly or the plucking of a male spider. As the American natural historian Henry

McCook wrote in relation to spiders and music: 'No doubt there is some similarity in the effects produced by the humming of insects' wings and the vibration of musical instruments'. There is a chain of membranes and threads, carrying the vibrations from one body to another: from the air passing through the vocal folds of my voice box, the skin of my throat, the thread of silk, the web of the spider, her claw on the web, to the slits in her legs. The experience of these sounds, however, differs between the spider and me. As with the use of spider egg cases in the acoustic instruments, the spider silk acts as a mediator, but one that both blocks and creates meaning. My serenade might have appeared to have the desired effect — the spider was drawn towards me. But it is a silent response. Somewhere along the chain of vibrations, my audible humming and singing was at the same time creating a sound inaudible to me — perhaps a fly, perhaps a male spider, or perhaps the singing of a teenage girl.

Seeing the spider's response was not enough, I wanted to be able to hear the sounds as she plucked at her web — to create a duet rather than a solo serenade. The vibrations of her web were too quiet for me to hear, so I had to find a way of amplifying them. I adapted a technique that I'd found in an old research paper from the 1970s, written by zoologists trying to measure the vibrations of a spider's web. I focused a small laser beam at the strands of web and on the other side was a photodetector. As the web vibrated, it would repeatedly break the beam of light going into the detector. That way, I could record the visible frequency of the vibrations and turn it into sound. I could hear the spider plucking its web in response to my own singing.[12]

Is this what the spider hears? Her vibrations reached me through a path of materials: from her plucking leg, through the silk, the laser, the

12 In 2015 the artist Tomás Saraceno used microphones to record the sound of spiders plucking their webs in response to musicians playing their instruments. Called 'Arachnid Orchestra. Jam Sessions,' live performances were held at the Centre for Contemporary Art in Singapore.

The vibrations of a spider plucking her web

photodetector, the electrical wires, the computer software, the sound speakers, the air, to my ears. It hints at a world of sound that is hidden to me, and to access it I must transform it. The spider and I are joined together through a path of vibrating silk, but we are hearing different things. Like the mysterious nyastaranga which was played by holding a spider web against a vibrating voice-box, the sounds of spider silk are not meant to be clear. It's a material primed for vibrations, that allows silent or invisible bodies to be heard.

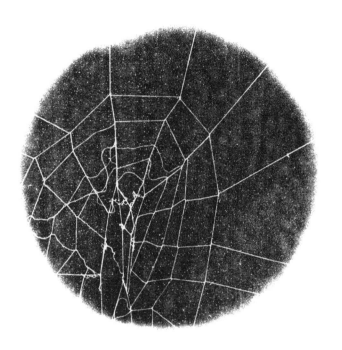

Transforming

Of bodies chang'd to various forms, I sing:
Ovid, Metamorphoses

I am on the roof of the Department of Zoology at the University of Oxford, inside a large humid greenhouse surrounded by hundreds of *Nephila edulis*, a species of golden orb spider. The close presence of these large spiders and their webs is not as disturbing as the thousands of flies that swarm around my face, unsettled by my arrival. A junior researcher accompanies me. One of his tasks it is to collect a bucket of maggots from the local fishing shop. He scatters these in trays on the floor of the greenhouse, where they hatch and feed on the rotting fruit laid out for them. On each web, hanging beside the female spider, is a neat line of fly carcasses along with the much smaller male spiders living off her catches. Ropes are strung up around the greenhouse to aid web building, at the corners of which are cocoons of silk containing spider eggs. Some have hatched into spiderlings, still grouped together in a scurrying bundle. These tropical spiders are provided for and protected from the elements, but they do have predators: native British spiders that hunt the *Nephila* spiderlings. The researcher spots one scurrying along the floor, and attempts to capture it. It escapes among the potted plants.

The spider greenhouse

These are the spiders of the Oxford Silk Group led by Fritz Vollrath. His group is one of a number across the world investigating the material of spider silk, and the possibility of creating synthetic materials that mimic some of its properties. After all, a material that entirely replicated a spider's dragline silk would mainly be of use to spiders. But a material that had the same strength and elasticity as spider silk, along with its lightweight properties, is of great interest — particularly if it can be produced on a commercial scale. It is not just the material itself that is the focus of research, but the way it is made; a spider can spin silk at ambient temperature and low pressures, using only water as a solvent — all from the flies in its web. In contrast, a high-performance synthetic fibre such as Kevlar, which has a similar strength to spider silk, is made from petrochemicals that are put under high pressures and processed with strong acids. This process requires huge amounts of energy and creates toxic waste. If humans could imitate the spider's spinning process, it could dramatically reduce the harmful effects of industrial production on the environment. We could make in a way that was conducive to life.

This final story is about transformations. It's about spider genes inserted into other organisms, human cells bonding with silk, and the change from liquid to silken thread. But it's also about a subtle shift in biomaterial research over the last decade, from imitation to inspiration. If once the aim was to create a 'spiderless spider web' — a magical material that removed the troublesome presence of spiders — then this desire has been replaced by a focus on the spider's process of making. The material cannot be made without the process; as one researcher said, 'the secret's in the spinning'.

In 2012 a herd of goats living on a farm in Utah appeared on a BBC *Horizon* programme on biomaterials. These were no ordinary goats: they were spider-goats. Looking very much like a herd of goats — they neither clung to the ceiling nor scampered on eight legs — their 'spideriness' was contained within their milk, which once extracted and processed could be turned into threads of spider silk.

They were the descendants of the first spider-goat herd created over a decade before by the Canadian company Nexia. Founded in 1993 by Jeffrey Turner, a molecular geneticist based at McGill University in Montreal, the aim of Nexia Biotechnologies was to make materials using the biological processes of animals, such as their ability to make proteins in the form of silk in spiders, or milk in mammals. Turner believed that a biological 'factory' would offer a cheaper and more efficient alternative to current industrial methods. As he stated in a newspaper interview of 2002, 'In the future, animals will be our factories... Very cheap factories'.

Initially, Turner was interested in creating lactose-free milk, but when the funding for this collapsed, he turned his attention to the possibilities of creating an artificial spider silk. He contacted Randy Lewis, a geneticist who had recently isolated and cloned the genes for silk proteins from four types of spider silk. Turner believed that if the gene responsible for coding these proteins could be inserted into a more farmable animal than a spider, it would be possible to produce spider silk on a massive scale. He needed a living animal in which to insert this gene, and turned his attention to goats, whose milk, he believed, could be used as the vehicle for spider silk. Turner said at the time: 'It was a purely serendipitous find. The silk gland of spiders and the milk gland of goats are almost identical. Teats equal spinnerets'.

In 1998, Nexia imported 130 Nigerian dwarf goats from New Zealand. Unlike other breeds, these goats reach sexual maturity in three months, and are sexually active throughout the year. As Turner stated, the speed with which new dwarf goats can be bred helped Nexia to achieve its 'output potential quicker'. There was such excitement over Nexia's potential that from the initial funding of two million dollars from venture capitalists, in the year 2000 Nexia received $42.4 million from investors. The cost of research was high, but a commercial spider silk would be a hugely profitable material.

To create the transgenic goats, and ultimately the artificial spider silk, Turner used two species of spider: the European garden spider and the golden orb spider *Nephila clavipes*. The dragline silk of the *Nephila* spider is the benchmark material for researchers attempting to create synthetic spider silk — it is one of the toughest silks produced by spiders, and as such is the one against which the properties of synthetic silks can be measured. Researchers at Nexia took specimens of these two spider species, froze them in liquid nitrogen and then ground them into a powder. From this they extracted the spider gene that codes for spider silk proteins. All genes, including those in humans, contain the information for creating proteins, telling the body which proteins to produce and when. To prevent the spider silk gene from producing silk everywhere in the goat's body, a genetic switch was added. This meant that although the gene existed in all the cells of the transgenic goats, it would only trigger the production of spider silk proteins when it was in the mammary gland of a lactating female goat. The spider silk gene was inserted into a goat's egg and fertilised, creating a goat that in Turner's words was '1/70,000th spider'. The milk 'looks and tastes like the real thing' but once the fat was removed and the milk curdled by adding salt, the resulting residue could be diluted with water to form 'silk dope' — the name given to the liquid silk that a spider stores in its glands.

Turner now had the basic parts that he needed to make his silk. If he was a spider, his glands would be full of liquid silk, and he would be about to spin a thread. And this is where things became difficult. When a spider spins its silk, pulling a thread from its spinnerets, a range of complex processes is happening. Inside its abdomen are silk glands where protein molecules are secreted in the form of liquid silk. This leaves the spider's glands through silk ducts where water is removed and they emerge from the spider's spigots as solid or sticky thread. From here, the spider pulls and combines together the individual strands of silk.

If we zoomed into the silk proteins, we could see the chains of amino acids from which they are formed. A spider's dragline silk is made from only a few different amino acids, and these are arranged in quite short, repeating sequences. If the letter 'A' represents one amino acid, and the letter 'B' another, then their arrangement in the protein could look something like this: ABBAABBAABBA. If this chain were folded together like a very long snake of repeating 'ABBA's, then the 'A' on the top row would be attracted to a 'B' in the second row, which would be attracted to an 'A' in the third row and so on. Each row could bond to the next, making a very strong material. But these short repeats also have another effect. Because the sequence is repetitive, the individual protein molecules can slide and shift relative to one another and make new bonds between them. This sliding action may help to give dragline silk its elastic properties.

Turner may have replicated a silk protein, but the properties of spider silk lie in how the spider spins these proteins into threads. It is hard to ascertain exactly how Nexia spun their silk proteins. As one journalist wrote after a visit to the company, 'Turner volunteers only the barest details'. The spinning machine was described as an attempt to 'replicate the spider's anatomy' — one machine forced the dope through a tiny hole, from where it was stretched between two spindles to create fine threads. The secrecy surrounding this process is perhaps in part because Nexia was working in collaboration with the U.S. Army Soldier Biological Chemical Command in Massachusetts. Now renamed the Soldier Systems Center, this wing of the U.S. army is responsible for carrying out research and development into army equipment and materials with the aim of maximising 'combat effectiveness and survivability of freedom's defenders'. A material with the properties of spider silk is of particular interest to the military. Possible uses include tough, light skins for military equipment, and giant nets on aircraft carriers to stop planes as they land. Another reason for Turner's reticence was his intention to patent the silk-making process once he had perfected the method.

Nexia were able to create silken threads, which they named and registered BioSteel®. This new material did not match the properties of natural spider silk, having only 30% of its strength. In spite of this, in 2002 Nexia published its research and declared its project a success, both materially and financially:

'Where other scientists have tried but failed to mass produce or mimic spider silk, a super strong and supple creation, Nexia Biotechnologies has succeeded. "It's an immense achievement", says founder and president Jeffrey Turner. "When we announced it, our shares went up 40 percent in one day".'

The majority of written information on Nexia is from this period, between 2001 and 2002. Everything then goes quiet. Nexia's website, www.nexiabiotech.com, no longer exists. The events of the subsequent years can be found in the company's financial reports to their shareholders. It seems that only a few months after their announcement that they had produced artificial spider silk, Nexia had to lay off a third of their staff to save money because they were still unable to create an effective silk spinning process, and were therefore unable to create a marketable fibre. These problems continued, until by 2004 the company was running at a deficit of $48.7 million. In 2005 Nexia declared bankruptcy and sold its assets to PharmAthene, a pharmaceutical company based in Maryland.

Although Nexia disappeared, the herd of spider-goats went on breeding. They were eventually sold to Randy Lewis, the man responsible for providing the genetic code of the spider silk proteins, and now based at Utah State University. The spider-goats joined a range of biological systems that Lewis is using to create spider silk proteins. He has also implanted the spider silk gene into bacteria, silkworms and alfalfa beans to explore ways of producing different silk materials from spider silk proteins.

There is continued media interest in the spider-goats, but they have not yet produced a material that matches the strength and elasticity of spider silk. Articles written on artificial spider silk often describe unlocking the secrets of the spider, but one vital key remains unknown — the material transformation from liquid protein to solid silk as it leaves the spider's body. The mystery of how a spider creates its silk means that while the intention may be to create 'spiderless spider webs', the research depends upon becoming more and more involved in the lives and processes of spiders.

If spider silk research at the turn of the 21st century was all about biomimetics — attempting to synthetically replicate a natural material — then in the last ten years the focus has changed to bioinspired materials. A subtle difference, perhaps, but the complexity of the biological processes of making spider silk makes it unlikely that a synthetic silk that entirely imitates that of the spider can be produced. What *can* be attempted, however, is an exploration of a range of new materials that

draws inspiration from spider silk production — and to do this, more must be understood about the spiders.

The Oxford Silk Group define their work as bioinspired, as they are not aiming to exactly replicate spider silk, but to study the way in which the spider spins its web and use this as inspiration for developing new materials. One issue that Fritz Vollrath and his colleagues have highlighted is the difficulty of agreeing what a synthetic spider silk actually *is* — which of the many spider silks is being copied? Which of its properties? And does it matter how it was made? This lack of agreement among researchers over what would constitute a synthetic spider silk may explain the sporadic excitement in the media declaring that humans have made spider silk — certainly something from silk proteins has been made, but that doesn't make it the same as a spider's thread.

Rather than focusing on creating artificial spider silk, the structure of silk and its non-toxic production may offer sustainable ways of developing a range of biodegradable materials. To explore the spider's spinning process and how it affects the material, the researchers' initial stage is to collect silk proteins. These can be taken directly from the spider's silk glands and stored in the laboratory ready to spin, or they can be extracted from spider silk threads that have been collected from the spider and broken down into molecules, or living organisms are used as 'hosts' to produce the silk proteins, as in the example of the spider-goats. No one has synthetically produced a complete spider silk protein from scratch. The spinning processes that researchers then apply to these proteins are similar, involving the folding and stretching of silk dope into fibres, but there are subtle differences between the methods, and these are closely guarded secrets within the groups.

Vollrath and his collaborator David Knight founded the company Oxford Biomaterials Ltd to develop silk-based products for the biomedical industry. The focus of their work was to develop a process of spinning silk that would mimic that of the spider: a 'biomimetic spinning machine'. They extracted silk from a silkworm that had a similar amino acid sequence to that of spider silk but was easier to work with. They dissolved the silk under 'mild conditions' and refolded the proteins through a spinning process. The chemical structure may have been silkworm silk, but the process of making the material was inspired by the spider.

They named the resulting material Spidrex®. It is not confined to a thread, but may be used to create a variety of forms depending on the requirements, including sheets, gels and spheres. For example, it could eventually be cast into the shapes of joints to replace damaged cartilage or to be used as a structure to repair damaged nerves within the body. This potential links current research with the historical use of spider webs as a dressing for wounds. Spider silk is particularly effective for this, as it is anti-bacterial and biocompatible, which means it can be used inside the human body without being rejected. Recent research has found that human cells are particularly attracted to spider silk. Certain types of silk are known to bind integrins. Integrins are the molecules that enable the cells in our body to stick together — and account for the attraction of our cells to spider silk. This means that if we had silk inside our body, our cells would be drawn towards it and begin to grow along its structure. This is a far more intimate transformation than that of Spider-man. We will not be trying to imitate the spider; instead its silk will be drawing us in, cell by cell. Our bodies are not only compatible with spider silk, it seems that it may help us to heal and grow.

In the future someone may succeed in creating a mass-produced artificial spider silk, but the recurring headlines declaring that humans have finally made spider silk are resonant of the historical hopes for a spider silk industry to replace that of the silkworm: a burst of confidence followed by a quiet retreat. The properties of spider silk are so dependent upon the spider's spinning processes, there remains the enticing possibility that one cannot be replicated without the other: the desirable material of 'human spider silk' might only be made through a system of production that is conducive to life.

Continuous Making

I described the stories in this book as clues, *cliwen*: bundles of human and animal threads to be traced. As if by following them we might solve a mystery and come to the end of the story. But what happens instead is an expansion. Each tale and thread attracts more to the bundle. I start with what I think is a simple line of silk. I follow it down to the spider's spinnerets and am faced with hundreds of spigots making seven different threads, twisting and turning. Down into one of these spigots, I am in the silk ducts of the spider and she is pulling at the thread with her legs, layering together the chains of amino acids that link and fold into place. Out now, back into the open where with a wiggle of her abdomen she glues a sticky thread into place on the spiral of her web. And then she pauses. One of Mary Pfeiffer's girls gathers her up. She scrambles around the girl's hand, binding it in a trail of silk, until she is propelled downwards and hangs a few inches from the floor while her silk is slowly gathered on a metal clothes hanger. With a dot of shellac at either end, this silken thread is stretched across the eyepiece of a telescope down which the astronomer watches and waits for the Earth to turn, until 'click' — a star's path moves across the spider's thread. Now on a shelf, gathering dust, a spider bundles the thread into her jaws and the digested proteins form a new line of silk. With a tug, a passing breeze pulls the thread from her body and she takes to the air.

The things we make are tied to the stories we tell; ways of seeing and arranging the world that we share with others. And these stories are not entirely human.

When I began collecting spider silk to make into a glowing sculpture, the story I told myself was the one about the artist who transforms an unlikely, everyday material into something magical, valuable and lasting. Like an alchemist turning base metal into gold, I wanted to achieve something that had not been done before, and most importantly, to have it seen and recognised as such. These are (some) of the stories of art, particularly in western traditions: the transforming hand of the artist and the need to preserve objects.

But there are other stories and other ways of making. The consistency of the silk and what I could make was affected by the spider's age, diet and environment, but it was not just a material link. With each thread I collected, the story gathered to include the behaviour of the spiders as they made and remade their webs, the rhythm and seasons of their spinning, the different paths I walked to see their webs and my increasingly thready dreams. Set against my desire to create and display a finished object, I was faced with an animal that makes, ingests and remakes. This is what draws me back to spiders. It is not just the wonder of watching them weave webs or the remarkable structures that they create; it's the enjoyable discomfort of meeting with another way of being in the world — another way of making.

The Navajo people of Arizona and New Mexico have a practice they call Na'atl'o', which means 'continuous weaving'. It is a type of string game, similar to cat's cradle, used to tell stories of creation, history and the cosmos. The storyteller manipulates a string around their hands to create different forms: a star, an owl, a drum, a bow. These are not isolated representations, they are attached to stories and they are dynamic — with a flick of the fingers the string can transform between the hands into a bolt of lightning. The practice was taught to them by Na'ashjé'ii Asdzáá, the Spider Woman, and they can only be played in accordance with the life cycle of spiders. String games are played during the winter months, while the spiders are hibernating. If you play string games during the summer months when the spiders are carrying out their own weaving, you will be punished. A spider will come and urinate on you.

Making processes are complex. They are more varied than the narrow focus on what humans do with materials, or the even narrower focus on what artists do. The making of a thing depends upon material properties, the place in which it is made, the people making it, but it also depends upon what has gone before — forms and ways of thinking that echo down the centuries, and to which we must add the making processes of other living things.

As the spider silk tales in this book have progressed, the threads have become less tangible. Beginning with the spider-lines to map our location, to the weaving and layering of threads, to the audible and inaudible sounds of spider silk, we arrive at a place where the material of spider silk seems to exist in other organisms or in the human imagination. None of these stories are entirely in the past — spider silk continues to seduce, haunt and elude the desires of humans. Now, a broken gun-sight is about to be repaired with a thread of spider silk; the webs of the *Nephila* spider in the jungles of Malakula are about to be collected on bamboo canes; the spiders in the greenhouse in Oxford are waiting to be fed; and as you walk you're going to feel the brush of spider silk on your face.

Further Reading and Activities

Spider watching

In Britain lots of people like watching birds, bees and butterflies. Spider watching is less popular. There are obvious reasons for this, but I find that the more I know about spiders the less scared I am and the more I enjoy seeing them. If a house spider, *Tegenaria domestica*, is sitting in my bath it may look as though it is waiting with a malevolent plan, but it's probably a male spider that has worked up a thirst looking for a female. It is pausing for a drink of water on its way to drum on her web. I find this reassuring and curious — a peek into another animal's way through life.

Throughout the year spider species at different stages of their life cycle can be seen. Many hibernate or die over winter, but the *Zygiella* species can be found throughout the year. Their small orb-webs are easy to recognise, as they appear similar to the orb-webs of the garden spider, but with a section missing from the upper half — like a round cake with a slice taken out. In this gap will be a single strand of silk and if you follow this to the edge you will find a *Zygiella* spider waiting with its foot on the signal line.

In spring, the spiderlings of the garden spider will hatch into a pulsating ball of little orange spiders, and over the weeks they will send up their silk balloons and disperse in the wind. Gradually, over the summer, the spiders will grow with each successive moult of their exoskeleton until they become adults and ready to mate. This is usually when people are most aware of spiders in their gardens and houses — the spiders are at their largest, and the males are on the prowl.

I live in an apartment in the middle of a city. There isn't a huge variety of birds here, but there are lots of spiders to watch. There are at least 450 species of spider living in Britain, and sitting here on my two-metre square balcony I can see seven of them. Between each iron railing is the web of a *Zygiella* and there are four European garden spiders hanging on their webs stretched between pots and plants. I am particularly excited to see that a female *Araniella cucurbitina* has arrived. She looks very similar to a European garden spider — they're in the same orb-weaving family *Araneidae* — but instead of brown and orange patterning she is bright green with two stripes of red just above her spinnerets that look like a pair of lips.

Another spider to look out for on a hot summer's day is the jumping spider *Salticidae*. Unlike most spiders, it has excellent eyesight. It has four pairs of eyes, and the forward facing are noticeably large. It can move these up and down, left and right — following and focusing. As you approach it may turn its head to look at you and if it's interested, its body will then follow. If you want to interact with a spider, this is the one to look out for. Edging along a plant pot to my right is *Salticus scenicus* — the 'theatrical jumper'. It is striped black and white, so is also known as the zebra spider. Like other jumping spiders it moves in a skittish fashion, stalking its prey. Because of its movement it is perhaps the most kittenish of spiders and with its large eyes and slightly fluffy hair it also has the appearance of a kitten — albeit a very small one with eight legs. Once it's ready to pounce, it secures itself with an emergency thread of silk in case the ambush goes wrong. Then, it leaps.

Because their eyesight is so developed, the courtship rituals of jumping spiders are visual dances with some aural accompaniment. The dance movements are specific to each species. On seeing a female, the male will approach her in a zigzag pattern, raising his front legs in semaphore-like movements and vibrating his palps. The female will watch, or in some species she will join in the dance. In Australia the male peacock spider, *Maratus volans*, has a highly coloured flap on its back which it raises and shakes at the female while he claps his legs together.

On the bright red flower of a scabious plant sits a female crab spider, *Misumena vatia*. White, with long legs outstretched either side of her body, she crouches waiting for an insect to land. Then, she will pounce. This particular spider is not having much luck — it is not well camouflaged and stands out against the red of the flower. If I can see it, so can the insects (although not in the same colours — a bee, for example, might see a blue/green spider on a black flower). Normally, these crab spiders will wait on a flower that matches their own colouring — but what's extraordinary is that the females can also change their colouring to match the flower, from white to yellow to green. Red, unfortunately, is not one of their colours.

One of the most common spiders in Britain is the *Linyphiidae*, or money spider. These little brown or black spiders spin a horizontal sheet of silk, often in bushes or grass. Above this sheet are numerous vertical threads, which are used as supports and to trip up any passing insects. The spider hangs on the underside of its silken sheet, and when it senses prey it shakes its web so that the insect falls down to where it can bite it and pull it through the web. It mends any gaps in the silk sheet after it has eaten.

All of these spiders can be easily seen in the daytime, but for others I have to wait until the evening. I've developed a habit of going out on my balcony with a torch to look for spiders. Hidden species emerge from crevices and gaps in the wall. Behind me, in a hole where a drainpipe emerges from the kitchen, lives a female *Amaurobius similis*, a laced web spider. Its body is about a centimetre long; it is dark brown and shiny with a light patterning down its centre. Rather than making sticky silk, this spider makes a frilly silk known as cribellate, which acts like the soft side of Velcro — the insects are the hooky parts. At night it hangs on the underside of its web, but retreats into its hole during the day. If you can't wait until nightfall, spider hunters sometimes use tuning forks to tempt out the nocturnal species, but I'd recommend waiting until dark — their shine and patterning is particularly striking by torchlight.

Inside the apartment, house spiders occasionally appear, and the long-legged *Pholcidae* spider that shakes its web very fast if it's disturbed. But one of the most common 'spiders' is in fact not a spider — it is a harvestman, a different order of arachnid. These animals are the ones with tiny bodies but very long legs that hang around the walls. Unlike spiders, whose bodies look like they're in two parts, harvestmen appear to have just one main body. They also have just two eyes, rather than eight. Most importantly, unlike spiders, they cannot spin silk.

Recommended books and links

Written sources are listed in the bibliography. For a more general guide to spiders, I recommend the following:

The World of Spiders
William Syer Bristowe. London: Collins, 1958.
This is a classic book on spiders, published as part of Collins' New Naturalist series that aimed to encourage people to explore British wildlife. The beautiful covers of these books alone make them worth the search in second-hand bookshops, designed by the illustrators Clifford and Rosemary Ellis.

Spider Silk: Evolution and 400 Million Years of Spinning, Waiting, Snagging, and Mating
Leslie Brunetta and Catherine Lee Craig. New Haven, Conn.: Yale University Press, 2010.
An evolutionary guide to spiders and their silk, with detailed and clear descriptions on how spiders developed the ability to spin silk over 400 million years ago and how this evolved to the range of materials and uses that spiders demonstrate today.

Biology of Spiders
Rainer F. Foelix. Oxford: Oxford University Press, 1996.
This is a comprehensive study of spider biology, including their anatomy, webs, nervous system, behaviour and ecology and it is full of wonderful drawings, photographs and close-up images. The author also worked in the laboratory of Peter Witt — the man who drugged spiders.

Spiders of Britain and Northern Europe
Michael Roberts. London: HarperCollins, 1996.
This is a beautifully illustrated guide to almost every spider you might come across in Northern Europe, how to identify them by their appearance and webs, and even how to catch them. It is also full of clear and useful descriptions of spider morphology, communication and behaviour.

The British Arachnological Society website (britishspiders.org.uk) is an excellent resource for checking on spider identification, and has links with similar projects throughout the world. It runs a membership scheme for beginners and experts, and has set up an online spider recording scheme to try and map the distribution of spiders throughout the county. The International Society of Arachnology (arachnology.org) also provides up to date information on spider research, news and events taking place internationally.

Where to see spider web objects

Most of the objects mentioned are in museum storage, but there are some spider web objects on permanent display. These places are within striking distance of where I live and represent only a tiny fraction of what might be found in other parts of the world. In Chester Cathedral the cobweb painting of Madonna and Child by Johan Burgman can be seen, but as discussed this is probably painted on caterpillar rather than spider silk. The Africa Gallery (Room 25, display cabinet 11) at the British Museum has a spider web hat on display that was made in South Africa in the late nineteenth century (Inv. Af1910,–.125). The hat shape has been constructed with twigs and the spider web has been stretched onto this support, with the addition of some feathers. The Pitt Rivers Museum in Oxford has a Malakulan mask with spider web headdress on display in the Vanuatu section (Inv. 1899.62.391) and a spider web fishing lure made in Papua New Guinea (Inv. 1938.36.884). It also has a selection of duiker lures (Inv. 1938.34.667 and 668) and voice disguisers (Inv. 1938.34.454 and 464) on display. The Musée du quai Branly in Paris has a significant collection of works from Vanuatu, and Malakula in particular, on display in its Oceania gallery.

Bibliography

Written sources and personal correspondence are in addition to the general spider books outlined above and are listed in the order in which they are referred to in the text. All etymological definitions have been taken from the *Oxford English Dictionary*. Much of the research for this book is discussed in my PhD thesis, 'Making with spider silk: the entangled processes of human and nonhuman animals', University College London, 2013.

Introduction

Ovid. 'Ovid: The Metamorphoses Book VI', trans. by A.S. Kline. Poetry in Translation, 2000.

Mirfield, John. *John of Mirfield: Surgery: A Translation of His Breviarium Bartholomei*, trans. James B. Colton. New York: Hafner, 1969, 8.

Democritus. Fragment B154 cited in Jonathan Barnes, *The Presocratic Philosophers*. New York: Routledge, 2002, 355.

Seneca. Moral letters to Lucilius/Letter 121. *Selected Letters*. Oxford: Oxford University Press, 2010, 262.

Aristotle. *Aristotle's Physics: Books I and II*. Oxford: Oxford University Press, 1992.

Aristotle. *The Nicomachean ethics*, trans. by David Ross. Oxford: Oxford University Press, 2009.

Sorabji. Richard. *Animal Minds and Human Morals: The Origins of the Western Debate*. London: Duckworth, 1993.

Beginnings

Byatt, A.S. 'Arachne'. *The Threepenny Review* no. 78 (July 1, 1999): 20–23.

Hooke, Robert. *Micrographia*. London: J. Martyn and J. Allestry, 1665.

Heiling, A.M., and M.E. Herberstein. 'The Role of Experience in Web-building Spiders (Araneidae)', *Animal Cognition* 2, no. 3 (1999): 171–177.

Witt, Peter. 'Drugs alter web-building of spiders: a review and evaluation', *Behavioral Sciences*, 16 (1971).

Thomas, Dylan. *Under Milk Wood: a Play for Voices*. London: Phoenix, 1992.

Lining

Euclid, *The Thirteen Books of Euclid's Elements, Vol. 1*. New York: Courier Dover Publications, 1956.

Gascoigne, William to William Oughtred. 'Letter', February 1641. In Stephen Rigaud, ed., *Correspondence of Scientific Men of the Seventeenth Century*. Oxford: University press, 1841, 46.

Bedini, Silvio. 'Along Came a Spider — Spinning Silk for Cross-hairs: The Search for Cross-hairs for Scientific Instrumentation, Parts I and II', *The American Surveyor* (April 2005).

Turner, Steven. 'Spiders in the Crosshairs: Cobwebs, Instrument Makers, and the Search for the Perfect Line', *Rittenhouse : Journal of the American Scientific Instrument Enterprise* 6, no. 21 (1991): 1.

Herschel, William. 'Description of a Lamp-Micrometer, and the Method of Using It. By Mr. William Herschel, F.R.S.', *Philosophical Transactions of the Royal Society of London* 72 (January 1, 1782): 163.

Rittenhouse, David. 'New Method of Placing a Meridian Mark, in a Letter to the Rev. Dr. Ewing, Provost of the University', *Transactions of the American Philosophical Society* 2 (January 1, 1786): 183.

Maunder, Edward Walter. *The Royal Observatory, Greenwich; a Glance at Its History and Work*, London Religious Tract Society, 1900, 156–157.

'The Planet-Watchers of Greenwich', *Harper's New Monthly Magazine* I, no. II (July 1850): 234.

Darwin, L., Arthur Schuster and E. Walter Maunder. 'On the Total Solar Eclipse of August 29, 1886', *Philosophical Transactions of the Royal Society of London*. A 180 (January 1, 1889): 294.

Gerdes, Paulus. 'Symmetries on Mats Woven by Yombe Women from the Lower Congo: On the Interplay Between Cultural Values and Mathematical-technical Possibilities', in *Symmetry Comes of Age: The Role of Pattern in Culture*, ed. Dorothy K. Washburn and Donald Warren Crowe. Seattle: University of Washington Press, 2004, 83.

Schaldach, Karlheinz. 'The Arachne of the Amphiareion and the Origin of Gnomonics in Greece', *Journal for the History of Astronomy* 35, no. 4.121 (2004): 435–445.

Goldstein, Bernard R. and Alan C. Bowen. 'A New View of Early Greek Astronomy', *Isis* 74, no. 3 (1983): 336.

'200 Spiders Go on Strike, But Woman Coaxes 'Em Back', *New York Evening Mail*, August 21, 1915.

Schwind, Don. 'Spider Lady', *McCall's Magazine*, November 1940.

Will, Bob. 'Poisonous Spiders Give Woman Living': *Los Angeles Times*, November 16, 1952, 24.

Songer Hook, Nan. 'Spiders for Profit', *Natural History Magazine*, November 1955: 456–461.

Hannah, R. 'Black Widow Spiders Aid Sharpshooters', *Nation's Business* 30 (December 1942): 71–72.

Baird, E. and Nan Songer. 'Spiders for National Defense', *Scribner's Commentary* 11 (January 1942): 9–14.

Holland, Henriette. 'War-Working Spiders', *Travel* 83 (October 1944): 18–19.

'Spiders Spin for War', *Popular Science* 144, no. 3 (March 1944): 12.

Taylor, Alfred. 'Spiders' Jobs Hang by a Thread', *Yorkshire Evening Post*, January 23, 1967.

'The Use of Spiders' Webs in the Manufacture of Surveying and Astronomical Instruments', *Vickers News* (October 1931).

Personal correspondence:

Rebekah Higgitt and Gilbert Satterthwaite, email to author, March 25, 2013.

Tony Kay, interview by author, September 26, 2011. Selsey, West Sussex, transcript.

Weaving

Louise Bourgeois in interview with Robert Storr (c.1990), in *Louise Bourgeois* edited by Frances Morris and Marie-Laure Bernadec, London: Tate Publishing. 2007.

Hagy, James W. *Edge of America: folly beach a pictorial history*, Charleston: Shaftsbury books.1997.

Wilder, Burt G. 'How My New Acquaintances Spin', *The Atlantic Monthly* 18, no. 106 (1866).

Wilder, Burt G. 'The Practical View of Spider Silk', *The Galaxy*, July 1869: 101–102.

Bon de Saint Hilaire, François Xavier. 'A Discourse Upon the Usefulness of the Silk of Spiders. By Monsieur Bon, President of the Court of Accounts, Aydes and Finances, and President of the Royal Society of Sciences at Montpellier. Communicated by the Author', *Philosophical Transactions* 27, no. 325–336 (January 1, 1710): 2–16.

Réaumur, René Antoine de. 'Examen de La Soie Des Araignées Par M. de Réaumur', *Histoire de l'Académie Royale Des Sciences* 1710 (Paris 1732): 386–408.

Termeyer, Raimondo Maria de. 'Researches and Experiments Upon Silk from Spiders, and Upon Their Reproduction'. Translated and Revised by B. G. Wilder. Communicated to the Essex Institute. Extracted from the Proceedings, Vol. 5. Salem, Massachusetts, 1866.

Rolt, Daniel B. 'Letter from Mr D Bransdon Rolt to the Royal Society of Arts', November 29, 1830. Manuscript Transactions Vol 121 (1829-31) part 4 of 5. The Royal Society of Arts, London.

'Silk from the Spider', *Liverpool Mercury*, October 11, 1839.

Darwin, Charles. *The Voyage of the Beagle*, New York: Cosimo, 2010.

Jones, John Matthew. *The Naturalist in Bermuda: a Sketch of the Geology, Zoology, and Botany of That Remarkable Group of Islands; Together with Meteorological Observations*, London: Reeves & Turner, 1859.

'Natural History Column', *Nottinghamshire Guardian*, June 7, 1894.

'Spider Silk', *The Huddersfield Daily Chronicle*, April 27, 1891, 7405 edition.

'Spider Silk', *Glasgow Herald*, June 12, 1885, 140 edition.

'Stolen Spiders Web', *The Washington Post*, June 10, 1900.

'Training Spiders', *Los Angeles Times*, January 5, 1902.

'Fashions of the Day', *Daily News*, April 14, 1900, 16866 edition.

Peers, Simon. *Golden Spider Silk*, London: V&A publishing, 2012.

McCook, Henry Christopher. *American Spiders and Their Spinningwork: A Natural History* of the Orbweaving Spiders of the United States, with Special Regard to Their Industry and Habits, Philadelphia: H.C. McCook, 1889.

'Adina's Letter', *Cheshire Observer*, September 12, 1891.

'Spiders Weave Silk', *The Washington Post*, February 17, 1907.

'Veiling the Beautiful: Lines for the Ladies', The North-Eastern Daily Gazette, December 16, 1898.

Cooper Oakley, Mrs. 'How to Dress', *Woman's Herald*, October 17, 1891, 155 edition.

'Fashions-Society-Home Counsel', *Manchester Times*, August 18, 1899, 2193 edition.

Perrot, Philippe. *Fashioning the Bourgeoisie: A History of Clothing in the Nineteenth Century*, Princeton, NJ: Princeton University Press, 1994.

d'Aincourt, Marguerite. *Études sur le costume féminin, par Marguerite d'Aincourt*, Paris: E. Rouveyre et G. Blond, 1883.

Taine, Hippolyte. *Notes on Paris*, New York, 1875.

Ovid. 'Ovid: The Metamorphoses Book VI' trans. by A.S. Kline. Poetry in Translation, 2000.

Personal correspondence:

Simon Peers, interview by author, December 15, 2011. Victoria and Albert Museum, London.

Layering

Gell, Alfred. *Art and Agency: An Anthropological Theory*, Oxford: Clarendon Press, 1998.

Huffman, Kirk. 'Land of the Living Dead: Respect for the Ancestors in Southern Malakula, Vanuatu, Oceania', in *Overmodeled Skulls*, edited by Arthur C. Aufderheide, 17–75. Duluth, MN.: Heide Press, 2009.

Deacon, A. Bernard. *Malekula: A Vanishing People in the New Hebrides*, London: Routledge, 1934.

Deacon, A. Bernard, and Camilla H. Wedgwood. 'Geometrical Drawings from Malekula and Other Islands of the New Hebrides', *The Journal of the Royal Anthropological Institute of Great Britain and Ireland*, (January 1, 1934): 129–175.

Layard, John. *Stone Men of Malekula*. London: Chatto & Windus, 1942.

Layard, J.W. 'Degree-Taking Rites in South West Bay, Malekula. (With Plates XIV–XIX.)', *The Journal of the Royal Anthropological Institute of Great Britain and Ireland* 58 (January 1, 1928): 139–223.

Bonnemaison, Joël and Kirk Huffman, Darrell Tryon and Christian Kaufmann, ed. *Arts of Vanuatu*, Honolulu: University of Hawai'i Press, 1996.

Guidieri, Remo, and Francesco Pellizzi. 'Shadows: Nineteen Tableaux on the Cult of the Dead in Malekula, Eastern Melanesia', *RES: Anthropology and Aesthetics* no. 2 (October 1, 1981): 5–69.

Gell, Alfred. 'Technology and Magic', *Anthropology Today* 4, no. 2 (April 1, 1988): 6-9.

Bibliography

Barton, Gerry and Stefan J. Dietrich. *This Ingenious and Singular Apparatus: Fishing Kites of the Indo-Pacific.* Heidelberg: BoD — Books on Demand, 2010.

Cassirer, Ina. 'Paintings on Cobwebs', *Natural History Magazine* 65 (1956): 202–207/219–220.

Wiesend, Manuela. Tyrolean 'Paintings on Cobwebs': Technology and Materials', International Institute for Conservation of Historic and Artistic Works, 2012.

O'Reilly, Kira. 'Webskin Series: Felt Textures and Textual Feelings.' Kira O'Reilly, November 1, 2009. http://www.kiraoreilly.com/blog/.

Burton, Robert. *The Anatomy of Melancholy*, New York: New York Review of Books, 2001.

Personal correspondence:

Kirk Huffman, email to author, July 2, 2012.

Vibrating

Sappho, Fragment 31, cited in Roland Barthes, *A Lover's Discourse: Fragments*, New York: Hill and Wang, 1978.

Blackwood, B.M., and Henry Balfour. 'Ritual and Secular Uses of Vibrating Membranes as Voice-Disguisers', *The Journal of the Royal Anthropological Institute of Great Britain and Ireland* 78, no. 1/2 (January 1, 1948): 45–69.

Barth, Friedrich G. 'Spider Senses — Technical Perfection and Biology', *Zoology* (Jena, Germany) 105, no. 4 (2002): 271–285.

Barth, Friedrich G. 'Vibrations and Spider Behaviour', in *The 11th European Colloquium of Arachnology*, edited by J. Haupt, XI:10–22. Technische Universität Berlin, 1988.

Barth, Friedrich G., Ute Wastl, Joseph A. C. Humphrey, and Raghuram Devarakonda. 'Dynamics of Arthropod Filiform Hairs. II. Mechanical Properties of Spider Trichobothria (Cupiennius Salei Keys.)', *Philosophical Transactions of the Royal Society of London.* Series B: Biological Sciences 340, no. 1294 (June 29, 1993): 445–461.

Bastin, Marie-Louise. 'Musical Instruments, Songs and Dances of the Chokwe (Dundo Region, Lunda District, Angola)', *African Music* 7, no. 2 (January 1, 1992): 23–44.

Hunter, Linda. 'Transformation in African Verbal Art: Voice, Speech, Language', *The Journal of American Folklore* 109, no. 432 (April 1, 1996): 178–192.

Lifschitz, Edward. 'Hearing Is Believing: Acoustic Aspects of Masking in Africa', *West African Masks and Cultural Systems*, edited by Sidney L. Kasfir Tervuren: Musée Royale de L'Afrique Centrale, 1988: 221–230.

Lifschitz, Edward. 'Voice Disguisers', in *African Folklore: An Encyclopedia*, edited by Philip M. Peek. London, Taylor & Francis, 2003: 1011–1012.

Peek, Philip M. 'The Sounds of Silence: Cross-World Communication and the Auditory Arts in African Societies', *American Ethnologist* 21, no. 3 (1994): 474–494.

Hawkins, John. *A General History Of The Science and Practice Of Music: In Five Volumes*, London: Payne, 1776.

Capwell, Charles. 'Musical Life in Nineteenth-Century Calcutta as a Component in the History of a Secondary Urban Center', *Asian Music* 18, no. 1 (October 1, 1986): 139–163.

Clark, Linda L. *Women and Achievement in Nineteenth-Century Europe*, Cambridge: Cambridge University Press, 2008.

Transforming

Dyas, Matthew. *Horizon*: 'Playing God'. BBC, 2012.

Kaplan, David L. 'Spiderless Spider Webs', *Nature Biotechnology* 20, no. 3 (2002): 239–240.

Lazaris, Anthoula, Steven Arcidiacono, Yue Huang, Jiang-Feng Zhou, François Duguay, Nathalie Chretien, Elizabeth A. Welsh, Jason W. Soares, and Costas N. Karatzas. 'Spider Silk Fibers Spun from Soluble Recombinant Silk Produced in Mammalian Cells', *Science* 295, no. 5554 (January 18, 2002): 472–476.

'Natick | The United States Army.' Accessed November 29, 2012. http://www.army.mil/ info/organization/natick/.

'Nexia Biotechnologies.' Office of Technology Transfer, McGill University, October 30, 2002.

Osborne, Randall. 'Nexia Agreement For Asset Sale Awaiting OK From Shareholders | BioWorld', January 10, 2005.

'Oxford Biomaterials LTD: A Method of Spinning Spider-like Silk, the "Holy Grail" of Bio Materials.' Inside: Technology, www.ttp.com no. 8 (July 2012): 31–34.

Porter, David., J. Guan, and F. Vollrath. 'Spider Silk: Super Material or Thin Fibre?' *Advanced Materials* 25, no. 9 (2013): 1275–1279.

Vollrath, Fritz., D. Porter, and C. Holland. 'The Science of Silks', *MRS Bulletin* 38, no. 01 (2013): 73–80.

Vollrath, Fritz. 'Biology of Spider Silk', *International Journal of Biological Macromolecules* 24, no. 2–3 (March 1999): 81–88.

Vollrath, Fritz. 'Strength and Structure of Spiders' Silks', *Reviews in Molecular Biotechnology* 74, no. 2 (August 1, 2000): 67–83.

Vollrath, Fritz, Wayne J. Fairbrother, Robert J.P. Williams, Edward K. Tillinghast, David T. Bernstein, Kathleen S. Gallagher, and Mark A. Townley. 'Compounds in the Droplets of the Orb Spider's Viscid Spiral', *Nature* 345, no. 6275 (June 7, 1990): 526–528.

Vollrath, Fritz, and David P. Knight. 'Liquid Crystalline Spinning of Spider Silk', *Nature* 410, no. 6828 (March 29, 2001): 541–548.

Vollrath, Fritz, David Porter, and Chris Holland. 'There Are Many More Lessons Still to Be Learned from Spider Silks', *Soft Matter* 7, no. 20 (October 4, 2011): 9595–9600.

Vollrath, Fritz, and Paul Selden. 'The Role of Behavior in the Evolution of Spiders, Silks, and Webs', *Annual Review of Ecology, Evolution, and Systematics* 38 (January 1, 2007): 819–846.

'Synthetic Bioproducts Center — Utah State University.' Accessed November 29, 2012. http://sbc.usu.edu/htm/research/spiders.

Bibliography

Continuous Making

Carmean, Kelli. *Spider Woman Walks This Land: Traditional Cultural Properties and the Navajo Nation*, Walnut Creek: Rowman Altamira, 2002.

Wirt, W., M. Sherman, and M. Mitchell. 'String Games of the Navajo', *Bulletin of the International String Figure Association* 7 (2000): 199-214.

Acknowledgements

Writing this book was made possible by the generosity, support and enthusiasm of many — spider lovers and otherwise.

A big thank you to Mark Pilkington and everyone at Strange Attractor Press. It's been a pleasure. I would also like to thank Annie Blinkhorn, Georgina Tate and Linda Morgan for taking the time to read through the early drafts and for their responses.

My research has involved working with many archives and museum collections. I would particularly like to thank Sarah Walpole at the Royal Anthropological Institute, Anne-Marie Delattre at the Musée des Confluences in Lyon and Steven Turner at the Smithsonian Museum for all their help.

I am deeply grateful to the various spider silk people who were willing to share with me their research and ideas; their generosity helped to enrich this book. Thank you to Rebekah Higgitt, Chris Holland, Kirk Huffman, Tony Kay, Susanne Küchler, Kira O'Reilly, Simon Peers, Fritz Vollrath and the Oxford Silk Group, and Manuela Wiesend.

Thank you always to my family and friends for their continued support, interest and encouragement. My particular thanks to Elliot, Isabel, Dylan, Duncan and Romilly for keeping me informed of the activities of spiders.

Finally, thank you to Daisy Cleopatra and the spiders of Folly Island and thank you to Ed for the countless things and for not minding about the spiders.

Eleanor Morgan is an artist and writer. When she is not following spiders, she works with other artists and animals to rub fish, embrace sea anemones and make diamonds from the dead creatures of the River Thames. In 2013 she completed her PhD on the human uses of spider silk at the Slade School of Fine Art and the Department of Anthropology, University College London. She has exhibited and published her work in Europe and North America and is visiting lecturer at Kingston University and the Royal College of Art.

www.eleanormorgan.com